STAND YOUR GROUND

BUILD ACE CONFIDENCE AND SELF-ESTEEM
SURVIVE PEER PRESSURE AND BULLYING WHILE
STAYING TRUE TO YOURSELF

MIA REYES

© Copyright 2021 - **All rights reserved.**

The content contained within this book may not be reproduced, duplicated, or transmitted without direct written permission from the author or the publisher.

Under no circumstances will any blame or legal responsibility be held against the publisher, or author, for any damages, reparation, or monetary loss due to the information contained within this book, either directly or indirectly.

Legal Notice:

This book is copyright protected. It is only for personal use. You cannot amend, distribute, sell, use, quote, or paraphrase any part, or the content within this book, without the author or publisher's permission.

Disclaimer Notice:

Please note that the information contained within this document is for educational and entertainment purposes only. All effort has been executed to present accurate, up-to-date, reliable, complete information. No warranties of any kind are declared or implied. Readers acknowledge that the author is not rendering legal, financial, medical, or professional advice. The content within this book has been derived from various sources. Please consult a licensed professional before attempting any techniques outlined in this book.

By reading this document, the reader agrees that under no circumstances is the author responsible for any losses, direct or indirect, that are incurred due to the use of the information in this document, including, but not limited to, errors, omissions, or inaccuracies.

CONTENTS

Intro: You Don't Have To Bring Them Coffee	7
Who You Are Right Now	13
You And The Power Of Change	
Two Is A Crowd	23
Science, The Human Brain, And People Fighting The Same Fight As You	
The Clockwork Bully	33
Why Bullying Happens, How To Face It, And Success Stories	
Break The Cycle	61
Laying Your Stepping Stones	
Befriend A Million Mirrors	89
You, Your Body, And Your Self	
Step Outside Your Safety Net	103
Your Predictions And Fears Can Be Your Tools	
Create Your New Mindset Powerzone	125
Your Strength, Your Decisions, Your Power	
Get The Most Out Of Change	141
Standing On Firm Ground	
Kudos: Look How Far You've Reached	155
References	159
Image References	175

Don't Forget Your Free Gift!

Enjoy this **MindArt Collection** of images proven to calm or elevate your mood! This is based on real human psychology studies, like the psychology of colors and cognitive auto-response to scenery and texture.

As proven in countless scientific studies, images and art can affect emotions, change perspectives, and calm or energize mindsets in almost everyone. So whenever you need to take 5, reset your mindset, cool down a little, or sort out racing thoughts, find your perfect image to set the stage.

All images are free to download and use as you please. They make awesome desktop art, wall art, and will look amazing on any vision board!

Scan the Qr code below or pick up your free copy of the collection here: www.mia-reyes.com

INTRO: YOU DON'T HAVE TO BRING THEM COFFEE

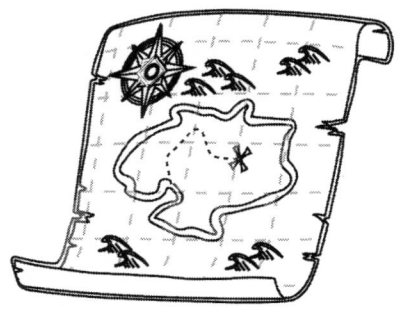

Have you ever wondered what it would be like to take the lead? Or what it feels like to stand firmly behind your idea even when others think they know better?

It's so much easier said than done.

Even if you often dream about being brave and assertive, in real life it often seems much safer to go with the crowd. To keep your ideas quiet. To let others decide.

Inside though, it's a different story.

You know your idea was way better. Or you might get a gut feeling something's off. Should you really be joining in? Are you unsure if you agree? Shouldn't you say something, or even just grab your best friend and leave?

When it comes to dealing with, well... *life*, we're always told to stand our ground. Sure, it sounds great, but realistically, it's often really hard to actually gather the guts and do it.

You might be feeling insecure, not too confident, scared to say what you really think, or anxious about what everyone else will think about you. How could you stand up to all these main characters, when you're feeling nervous just being in their presence? And that's when it gets truly frustrating. You know all the shoulds, and should-have-dones, yet it just seems impossible to react how you want when it counts. And how do you know your intuition is even right?

Maybe you often wake up dreading the day because someone at work or college likes to take advantage of you. Maybe they ask you to make them coffee which definitely isn't in your job description. Like when I was a junior at a corporate office, and someone in my team (honestly, just barely above me in the office hierarchy) kept asking me every single day to go to the printer and bring her the documents she just printed. Or maybe, they always steal your notes you worked so hard to finish last night, and use them as their own.

Sounds similar to what tends to happen to you?

If it does, then I want you to know you can make things change. And yes, this is definitely also one of those *should*s. Because these frustrations and blocks are pushing you down, and freezing your confidence below sea level. Which is why you don't feel strong enough to stand your ground when it counts.

I used to be quite insecure too. From being picked on as the new kid at a new school, to trying for years to win over a friend who liked to choose a different bestie every week, I wasn't always too socially confident either. Once, a boyfriend I was really into told me I was following him around like a sick puppy. I was around 20 by then.

I'm kind of grateful to him though, because that was my wake up call.

So, no matter where on the self-esteem scale you are at this moment, there is a way to feel more grounded and stronger. And I'm proud of you for wanting to make a change. Your decision to make this effort is a big deal. It's like you've just picked up the first big rock blocking your way and threw it away.

Next!

Feeling insecure, hesitant or afraid can manifest itself in many different ways.

You might seek approval from other people all the time. You might worry so much about other people's opinions, that you often step back or stay quiet just for the fear of other people's judgment. On the other hand, getting compliments is also awkward. You often don't know how to respond.

Maybe you always doubt your decisions. Where others welcome a wide variety of choices, you feel overwhelmed. If you choose one, how do you know you won't miss out on the other? And despite all of these doubts, you might still expect yourself to be perfect, and when you aren't, you feel defeated.

It's exhausting.

But, there's a way out. And the good news is, the more you're struggling right now, the stronger your motivation to find the exit can become.

Seriously! Trouble, discomfort, pain, struggle, and the way they feel can often be the world's strongest motivators.

So if you're tired of feeling like a bamboo stalk in the wind, and being dragged back by negative thinking, remember that feeling. Engrain it as deep in your brain as you can. Then, use it to your advantage. You want to change it. You never want to feel like this again.

That's your bottom line.

Now, let's see what you'll discover in this book.

First, you will learn the reasons behind the things troubling you right now, to give you a better sense of why they have been happening. Then you'll learn to build a stronger mindset as a base for more stability and higher self-confidence.

You'll learn how to give less power to the tendencies to doubt, underestimate, and criticize yourself, and more power to your own reasoning and thinking processes. You'll learn to respect your decisions and the successes and mistakes that emerge from them.

While working on your progress, you'll gradually start feeling confident enough to speak up when it's due, choose what *you* want to do, share your opinions, stand up to bullies and people who want to project their own insecurities on you. By focusing on yourself, your inner voice will change into one that offers kind, compassionate, and loving words instead of criticisms.

You'll move your life forward.

As long as you are willing to put in some hard work, and make yourself a priority as you move through the process, you will create the life you've been dreaming of.

Doesn't that sound amazing?

It won't happen easily or fast, and you will have to challenge yourself a fair bit along the way. But, if you can turn your life around, all those efforts will have paid off in the end. So, when you're ready, let's start!

WHO YOU ARE RIGHT NOW

YOU AND THE POWER OF CHANGE

Right now, you're probably stuck between wanting to change, and not really knowing how to change.

What's the next step? What if I fail? Who will be the first to say "I told you so"?

Thoughts like this will keep racing around in your head a lot, especially in the beginning. The most powerful first step you can take is to accept they're there, just for now, and then try anyway.

Think about the last time you were faced with a decision or a dilemma, one where you had to choose between what you want and what your friends want—only to end up going with their choice.

Does this happen way more often than you'd like?

Do you always find yourself agreeing with other people just to avoid conflict?

Maybe you really don't want another drink, but it's easier to say yes, to keep a low profile. Even if the hangover is frustrating the next day. You don't want them to label you as a lightweight. That's called adjusting to peer pressure. Doing things to blend in.

But… Why does it keep happening?

So many times you just *know* what is right. Because it's what your heart and mind tell you. But then you suddenly lose your nerve. Especially when you're hanging out with the most popular person you know. You just don't want to put a foot wrong. The familiar doubts creep in, and make your confidence waver. However, deep inside you also know this is not ideal, and that you don't like the feeling of letting your judgment be manipulated by these doubts, or by someone else, no matter how high up the social ladder they are. You just wish you were strong enough to say no, or stay true to what you really think.

In a study at the University of Wisconsin, two-thirds of students identified peer pressure and the projection of gender stereotypes as one of the hardest things they had to face as a teenager.

Well, the fact there's a scientific definition for what you're feeling, and also research studies involving hundreds of students, shows that many other people are dealing with the same thing.

So if you've been under the suspicion that you're the only one watching other people get what they want, while your own life is frozen still, it's simply not true. There are other human beings who feel exactly the same. And they all have the amazing ability to change it.

So do you.

It just takes some realization, some self-discovery, and a sprinkle of compassion and patience with yourself.

Once you discover that power and learn how to use it, standing up for yourself will come a lot more naturally.

I know this because I used to be there too. Since the kids at my new school didn't welcome me that easily, I'd sign up for things I wasn't really interested in, just to try and fit in. I wanted to be part of the main group. I competed for the attention of people who weren't really all that interested in me. But later on, I realized I can find my own things to be good at, my own style, my own interests, and make far more genuine friends that way.

It's totally possible. But you do need to navigate through a few shifts first.

Your Starting Point

Learning to understand your starting point is a huge part of the process, and a significant addition to the foundation you'll be building on. Even though reflections are probably quite uncomfortable and can be painful, they need to happen in order for you to move on. Like when you have a ghost, you need to acknowledge its presence first, and only then you can release it and let it find solace (...ugh, it's nearing Halloween as I write this).

Bearing this in mind, let's take a little quiz. Staying as honest with yourself as you can, tick off any of the following points that ring true (or sometimes true), to you:

- You often don't speak up because you're scared of rocking the boat.
- You tend to say sorry quite a lot. Sometimes you're not even sure what you're saying sorry for.
- You're unsure if you deserve recognition, even

though in reality you work twice as hard compared to the rest of your mates.
- You find it hard to define and set up boundaries.
- You feel guilty when you prioritize your needs, feelings, or wants before those of your friends.
- You are always overthinking even seemingly tiny, everyday decisions.
- Once you do make a decision, you often end up regretting it later.
- You don't feel like you deserve compliments.
- You do people a lot of favors, without getting appreciation or favors back.
- You're acting or posing quite often, because you think people wouldn't like the real you.
- Your own mind often seems to be your most bitter critic.
- You tend to take innocent things personally, like when a friend genuinely doesn't have time to grab the usual lunch with you this week, you see it as rejection.
- You over-justify your actions, both to yourself and to others.
- Fidgeting is your thing.
- You might adjust your opinions often, to fit any particular group of people you're with.
- It's often difficult to trust your own thinking and decision making process.
- Negativity seems to have this weird superpower to completely overturn your day in a flash.

Add anything else you might have noticed while thinking about this:

- ……………………………………………………………………
- ……………………………………………………………………

And done! Great work. It doesn't matter too much how many you ticked or didn't tick. What does count is honesty, and looking into the reality of your personal experience.

Of course, being genuine with things that are difficult to face or answer is a grind! But by reflecting on these tough points you now have a better perspective of your starting point, and of approximately where on the self-esteem scale you are at the moment. Take some rest if you need to. You deserve it!

Change Changes Everything

Fast backward a few months when I was still fully immersed in research, I was making a huge point of chatting to people wanting to share stories about their past struggles and the various fights they put up to overturn their bad luck.

And whatever happens, I'll never forget talking to one girl in particular.

She was amazingly confident and positive despite having a disability. You'd find it hard not to feel uplifted by her refreshing attitude and just… general loveliness. So when we finally ordered oat-milk cappuccinos and she opened up about her story, I didn't expect to hear what I did.

At college she was a target of bullies. Back then, she was often self-conscious and felt embarrassed about her condition, so she preferred to keep quiet and just get on with her studying without getting involved in anything else. For this, a couple of other students picked her out, and tormented her, sneakily, secretly, and out of sight.

She was too scared to say anything. She spent months in hiding, constantly glancing over her shoulder. Until she finally told a friend and together they decided enough was enough.

Feeling safer now her friend had her back, she reported the case.

Next, it was time to build up her resilience and learn to be more assertive. She was so desperate to move away from giving her condition so much importance in her own mind. She wanted to feel more comfortable in her skin everyday. She was tired of associating her disadvantage with defeat. There must be a way.

Sitting across from me sipping hot coffee and talking about such a heart wrenching experience in such a genuine way, it was pretty clear to me she had succeeded on her quest.

She went on to share the steps she felt were the most significant in fuelling her search for inner strength:

- She started by booking 8 sessions with a therapist. Booking a few sessions in bulk ensured she couldn't chicken out so easily (exact words), but also meant

she didn't feel overwhelmed by signing up indefinitely.
- She joined a local social enterprise (like an evening club), which focused on disadvantaged young people, providing them with space and ideas to explore their creativity, their potential, and most importantly giving them the opportunity to talk and support each other.
- That's when she discovered she enjoyed focusing on positivity and encouraging others in exactly the same way her friend had once encouraged her.
- She read a ton about self-compassion and body positivity, and learned to point out the things she liked about herself more.
- She focused on small challenges at the start. It's so easy to be intimidated by huge goals that are too far out of reach (for now). So, with the help of some other people from the social enterprise group, they would set two realistic challenges for each other every week. And so many of them were successful! Each victory was a stepping stone, and each try was proof they were growing stronger.

That afternoon before heading back to the station, she asked me to tell you her story is also your story. You can lift yourself up. She believes in you. And so do I.

If she was able to turn her life around despite the unfair hand she was dealt, you can do it too. It is possible to find a way out even from a proper deep-gutter situation.

The process is a mixture of major self-discoveries, reflections, hearing about other people's experiences, and challenging yourself to grow equally well from both your successes and your mistakes. All this will help you awaken the confidence that's currently stuck tapping the snooze button. But, if it also sounds quite overwhelming to you right now, that's totally fine because we will start with small steps as well.

There is so much more for you to explore. But taking it slow is taking it smart. So for now, just keep turning the pages.

TWO IS A CROWD

SCIENCE, THE HUMAN BRAIN, AND PEOPLE FIGHTING THE SAME FIGHT AS YOU

People who have healthy self-esteem hold themselves in high regard and have positive thoughts about themselves. They are also quite optimistic about life. When they face a challenge, they take responsibility for making a decision, and are confident enough to (mostly) stick with it. They know their value and aren't afraid to take a stance when it matters.

Maybe, right now you think you couldn't possibly be further away from becoming that kind of a person.

If this is how you feel, remember you weren't born that way. Nobody is born with either high or low self-esteem. While growing up, our self-esteem develops based on the experiences we have, the people we meet and share our lives with, the communities we are part of. If you grew up being constantly challenged, had a traumatic experience or struggled with lots of problems, the reason why you're currently feeling the way you do is most likely lurking somewhere in that past.

For me, it's those experiences that I can still vividly remember today, and by now I've been able to pinpoint some of the roots leading to my past insecurities. And I most certainly got many things wrong. I also did things I now wish I could take back. Just because they weren't very self-respectful. But, I also know that a rough learning curve is still a learning curve. Nobody is ever perfect and stumbles are part of everyone's life.

And I'm positive that soon, you will start seeing the lessons and the messages behind the things you have been going through as well.

What Happens In Your Brain?

Now, if you ask a psychologist what causes low self-esteem and insecurities, they will tell you it all develops as you form negative thought patterns which are hard to get out of. They are repetitive, super resistant, and keep nagging and nagging until you start perceiving them as the truth.

You might start criticizing yourself a lot more, develop fears, or make negative predictions about things, which then make you too afraid to even try, and so you resort to safety behaviors and avoidance behaviors instead (more about these two disguised traps later).

And before you know it, you've built a giant, padded, bouncy comfort zone fortress where you plan to stay for the rest of your life.

This is nothing to be ashamed of. Again, if a psychology expert can name it, it means a lot of other people have experienced it too, and many other people all over the world are literally fighting the same fight as you right now. Also, many of them will be able to win it.

Have you ever wondered what happens in your brain when you're dealing with insecurity or are going through that sudden but intense burst of negativity?

According to a study, people who experience fluctuation in their self-esteem are often prone to other challenging cognitive signals too, like symptoms of anxiety or depression (Geert-Jan, W., et. al., 2017). Their mind generates more prediction error responses in their insula, the part of the brain that is responsible for self-esteem along with part of the prefrontal cortex. This simply means that having low self-esteem may be a potential neurobiological marker that can develop into further issues.

This is also how your brain creates those subconscious patterns, and the safety behaviors that are so hard to break once they've made themselves at home. Often, you won't even know that you have developed these behaviors until they start interfering with your life. Like if you're worried what your friends would think about you taking dance classes, you won't sign up even though you really want to.

In a nutshell, safety behaviors work as a quick fix to prevent fears from coming true, but they come at a cost. While these safety and avoidance habits might make you feel safe for a while, they don't actually solve anything. Not in the long term at least.

Actually, they might have serious potential to make you even more frustrated and more anxious. So if you're unsure whether something you're (not) doing is an avoidance behavior, ask yourself:

- Am I afraid something bad will happen if I don't do this?
- How anxious would I feel if I couldn't do this?

Again, recognizing the why and trying to point out the reasoning behind will help you stay more mindful of any avoidance or safety behaviors you might be doing repeatedly, and to address them in the future.

You might have also heard before that self-esteem and self confidence are actually two slightly different things. While self-esteem is how you see yourself and your value, self-confidence is the belief you have in your abilities and skills.

Throughout this book, we'll talk a lot about how to improve both. But always remember, if you feel like you could do with more support, opting in for some professional help is always a great option.

The most common and effective therapies are competitive memory training (COMET) and cognitive behavioral therapy (CBT). Both these methods have been super useful for many people and can also help with other things like social anxiety. Even though seeking professional help might seem scary at first and it can take a lot of courage to do, it has the potential to become a giant stepping stone. We'll talk about all this in much more detail later.

All About Self-Confidence And Self-Esteem

Now, the great thing is that both self-confidence and self-esteem are considered skills. They are attributes that you can learn, practice, and improve. And once you start working on making them both stronger, amazing things will happen.

You'll find it easier to trust yourself and your decisions, which will open your life to more opportunities. You'll be able to express yourself more freely, stand behind your opinions, you'll recognize when it's time to speak up and won't feel afraid to let your voice be heard by others. That said, you'll also see more clearly when it's better to stay quiet and make a swift exit. Your friends will notice this, and will be more open with you as well.

You won't feel so hindered and frustrated by fear. It will become easier to let things go. You'll let yourself explore the things you're interested in and excited by.

That's a lot to look forward to!

Here are some pointers to get you started:

- Make a start on transforming your perception of yourself into a positive one. It might be hard to get used to, especially if you've been feeling quite negative, but take little steps, and let them become bigger as you go. For now, make an effort to just notice and acknowledge one positivity a day. Something you secretly know you're good at. Something you made that turned out excellent. Notice any small successes, breakthroughs, moments you made someone laugh, or a good hair day. Positivity can also create a brain pattern. Will you help it happen?
- Think about your values and make these your priority. Think about what you want to achieve on a personal level, studying, or professionally. They will change as you go, but learn to always keep them at the back of your mind, and at the forefront of your actions whenever it's possible.

- This might sound strange, but get to know yourself a bit more. And I mean the real you. The you only you understand. Chances are there's a lot happening in the background, which you might have noticed only briefly, or can't quite name yet. It used to happen to me a lot (and still does), and it's why I love *16 Personalities*. Seriously, it's the most fun and useful personality test out there. You take the free test, learn which one of the 16 personality types you are, and get a full breakdown of your character traits. They even give you a list of famous real and fictional characters you share your personality type with, which is excellent. I couldn't quite believe how accurate my results were, and it helped me understand some things about myself a lot more. Ok, I'll share! My personality type is Advocate, INFJ-A. And apparently I share this type with Marie Kondo, Morgan Freeman, Atticus Finch, Jon Snow, and Aragorn. Cracking!
- You can find *16 Personalities* here: https://www.16personalities.com

These exercises serve as awesome pick-me-ups you can use to kickstart the process of building up the self-knowledge and confidence you need in your life right now.

Inspiring People Are Everywhere

Stories are incredibly powerful. And the people who tell them? Even more so.

Everyone can experience things similar to what you're going through right now, no matter their background, where they are now, or how successful they are. Noone is immune from the potential of experiencing serious setbacks.

And just like you, everyone has the ability and the strength within them to flip their life around.

Like Gavin. His father suffered from manic depression and so Gavin grew up being scared a lot, often hiding. Although his mom tried her best to contradict the negative outbursts, Gavin ended up with low self-esteem and social anxiety issues. He never felt like he fitted in anywhere, especially at school. And when someone criticized him, he took it personally each time. This continued until he was older, and his adult life was still affected so heavily he wanted desperately to try and change. So he challenged himself to start doing at least five things differently. He stopped drinking (one of his safety behaviors), created a morning routine with journaling, set clear career goals at work, meditated every evening, and practiced visualization techniques. It took a few months to see results, but he enjoyed every minute of it. His efforts paid off as he felt more assured of his abilities, and finally had the space to be himself.

I've also heard from a student who suffered from low self-esteem at her new college. She couldn't focus, couldn't connect with others, couldn't bring herself to try any new things, and completely lost her desire to learn. I was so glad when at the end of her email she described how she took a stand by reaching out to a professional and trying CBT therapy. She learned a lot from the treatment, but she said the key to her success was definitely the first step—making that huge decision to change things.

Another person who admitted she struggled with low self-esteem a lot is Angelina Jolie. She might seem like the most confident person in the world (after all, she is Angelina Jolie) but she wasn't always like that. When she was young, she found it extremely difficult to connect and make friends because she was different. She went through some pretty harsh coping strategies, which in reality weren't coping strategies at all, and in fact kept making things worse. Eventually, with help and a big serving of determination she was able to stop falling, and climb back, and become a successful woman who always fights for good causes.

Russell Brand was a surprise to read about. He always came across as rather self assured to say the least. But he actually had self-esteem issues from a young age and later developed an eating disorder. Then he also reached the point where he realized that he didn't want to be crushed by life. He knew he was tough and he proved himself right. Now, he is one of the most confident people out there and it's always refreshing to witness how he is able to laugh at himself without spiraling back into the darkness he had to deal with in the past.

As you can see, people from all walks of life can struggle with all sorts of insecurities. But people from all walks of life can also overcome them.

And you have that power too.

THE CLOCKWORK BULLY

WHY BULLYING HAPPENS, HOW TO FACE IT, AND SUCCESS STORIES

So... How are you?

I hope you are feeling more inspired and encouraged than when you began. And before we dive into the next chapter, feel free to take five.

If you want, color the mandala on the next page to help you sort out your thoughts.

Now, if you're someone who has been affected by bullying, and may not feel like going through this chapter alone, feel free to skip for now and wait until you can read it with a friend, a family member, or someone else you trust.

But it is an extremely important topic to talk about. So whenever you're ready, let's take a deep breath and get through this together:

By definition, bullying means repeated verbal or physical aggression towards a person. When people hear the term bullying, they often think it only affects kids and teenagers. And it often does. But it's also true that it commonly happens to young adults, adults, and in fact people in every age group.

It can happen anywhere. At college, at the workplace, at the bus stop, online.

Here are the most common types of bullies:

- Secondary bullies who join in to avoid being the next target.
- Narcissistic bullies who put other people down to feel superior.
- Physical bullies who do things like stealing, hitting, invading people's personal space, threatening physical harm, stalking.
- Verbal bullies who use words to make other people feel miserable.
- Workplace bullies who spread rumors, demotivate, conspire, or exclude people from projects and work events.

All of this is extremely upsetting and hard to deal with. Where do you even start? People affected are often too scared or too embarrassed to say anything. But bullying is possible to overcome, and many people have successfully done so. There are many ways you can approach this, get through, and come out on the other side full of strength, resilience, and compassion.

First, it helps to try and understand the issue a bit better. You need to know what you're up against to make a plan. And that's exactly what we'll be doing here.

Myths About Bullying

If you're someone who has been going through bullying, you might have wondered sometimes if you're to blame for any of it.

Absolutely NOT.

Becoming a target is not your fault, and never will be, no matter how you look at it. But why does it happen then? In this chapter, we will try to get as close to the bottom of this as we can. Let's start by deconstructing some of the common myths:

Myth: All bullies have self-esteem issues or they are born as bullies.

Some people think bullies feel bad about themselves and that's what makes them lash out at other people. While this is definitely true for some, it's not the case for everyone. Many bullies are socially successful and self-confident. They might use bullying to gain more power, or simply to get what they want through the people they work with, or are in a relationship with.

Bullies aren't born that way either. Often, they learn bullying behaviors while growing up. Some of them might have been bullied in the past, and then they do it to others without really knowing why. Or they do it to re-establish themselves back into a hierarchy or a dynamic.

Myth: Bullies don't have friends because they're loners.

There are always exceptions, but for the most part this is another myth. Often, bullying happens because the person craves social power. And bullying others somehow makes them more popular (I know, it's messed up!). Sometimes, the entire group then gangs up on one person together.

Myth: Bullies stop when they grow up.

Sadly this isn't always true. When kids bully others they'll often do it as adults too. Either that or they still use negative language and behaviors to get attention. Unless some sort of intervention happens while bullies are still young which helps them eliminate the bullying behavior, they often continue on.

Myth: Only people with a victim personality can be bullied.

There are certain things bullies notice and use, like being withdrawn or shy. But this doesn't mean that such people have a victim personality. Also, bullies don't always choose people with these traits. Literally anyone could be a target depending on the bully's personal motives. This is what makes it all so unpredictable.

Myth: Being bullied makes you stronger.

No it doesn't. In fact, many people end up losing a part of themselves because of bullying. They suffer socially, emotionally, and physically. They often feel isolated and lonely, develop anxieties and fear. If anything can be granted in this regard, it's OVERCOMING bullying that makes people stronger, not the bullying itself.

Myth: Bullying is easy to notice.

Wouldn't it be much easier if other people realized others were being bullied straight away? They could then reach out and help early on. But the reality is, bullies look like normal people and often blend right in. And they can be so sneakily smart too. They know exactly how not to be discovered. They use people's emotions to work in their favor, making them scared or ashamed to speak up. Which is why bullying isn't always easy to spot.

Myth: Speaking up will make things worse.

Many victims of bullying believe that speaking up will make matters worse. But it doesn't have to be that way. Speaking up doesn't always mean running straight to HR. It can mean talking about your situation with someone you trust first, someone who you know will be able to help you solve the issue or get the support you need to put an end to the situation. You'll feel so much better when a friend has your back. You can then refer to school or workplace policies together, and come up with a plan such as always going places together for the next few weeks, while things are being dealt with.

Myth: Being bullied is normal.

It can be common, but it's definitely not normal. In fact, some types of bullying are literally against the law.

If you notice someone being bullied, one of the best things you can do is reach out to them and work together to help that person overcome the situation.

Bullying is a real problem no matter who or where you are. Global research has shown that approximately 23% of all college students have experienced bullying, while approximately 19% of young professionals have been affected by it in the workplace. And while no one deserves to be part of that statistic, it does show we are not alone, we are not weird, and we sure as hell aren't weak.

Cyberbullying

Cyberbullying happens when one person inflicts humiliation or emotional pain on another using technology. It could be posting embarrassing photos or personal information about another person on social media without consent, sending intimidating and unsolicited messages on chat, harassment, blowing up drama about another person's behavior, habits or appearance, spreading hate, posting or forwarding personal communication, or sharing someone else's private details. Cyberbullying can also mean sending threatening or cruel text messages to people's phones, and unsolicited phone calls.

Cyberbullying has become one of the fastest-growing types of bullying in the world. It can happen to anyone with a social media account, an internet connection, or anyone with a phone, really. The most frightening power these trolls and keyboard warriors have over our sanity is that without much effort, they are able to get to us in our safe space, often literally invading our home with their toxicity.

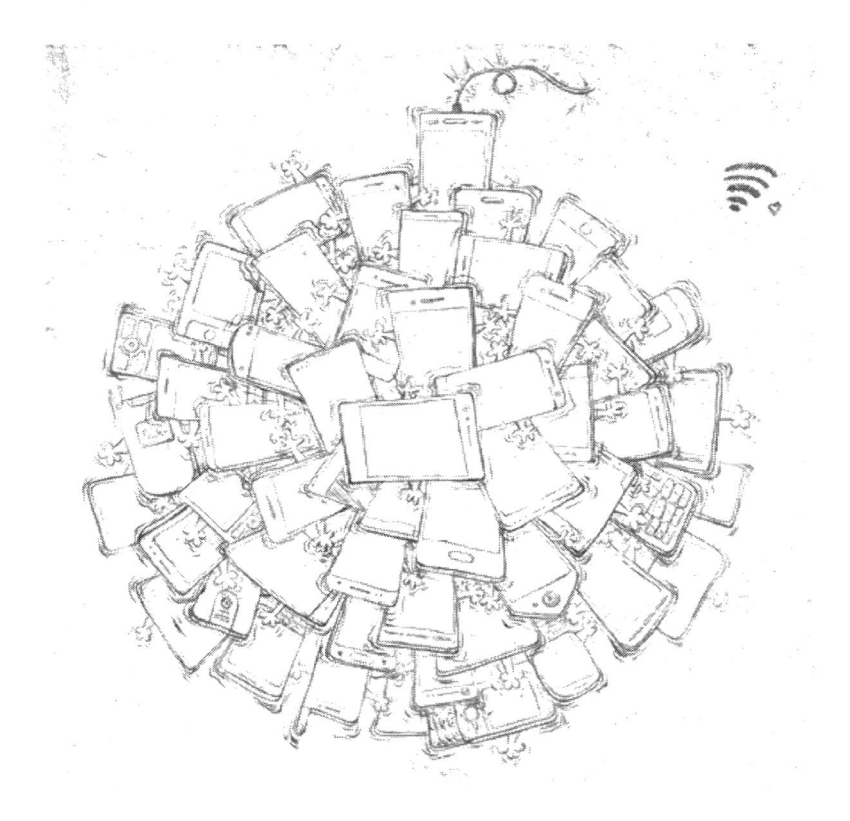

They can be extremely relentless. They can also find extremely effective ways to maintain anonymity, or steal other people's profiles, which makes things more difficult to deal with. Cyberbullying can also be much more challenging to notice, especially when adults like parents or teachers aren't active online.

So, contrary to what some skeptics still insist on saying, cyberbullying is real, it can happen to anyone, and it can have devastating effects.

If you're unsure whether someone online is bullying you or someone you know, here are a few basic questions to ask:

- Did you give consent to be contacted by this person?
- Have they suddenly switched from friendly to demanding?
- Does the interaction feel uncomfortable, forced, and awkward?
- Does this person know something personal about you and have they threatened to share it in any way?
- Do they keep messaging and calling you multiple times a day, even though you said you'd rather they didn't?

Don't accept it when people say cyberbullying is harmless and simply just ends when you sign out. That's not true. And it's why we have laws against cyberbullying too, which means if you can find out who is bullying you and prove that they have been harassing you online, the troll will face legal consequences. If you find yourself in a situation when a cyberbully has picked you or someone you know as their target, here's what you can do:

- Don't engage, or if you have been engaging, stop now. Of course it's natural to want to defend yourself, or set the record straight if they're spreading something untrue. But that's exactly what the troll wants you to do. By engaging you're only

fueling their fire. If there's one thing these trolls can't deal with, it's being ignored.
- Block the troll. Block them everywhere they might have access to your profile or pages.
- If they've been threatening you to expose some kind of personal information or photos, take screenshots of everything immediately, before they have a chance to delete the message threads.
- Record any unsolicited calls or Facetimes.
- Screenshot and collect any kind of tangible evidence, like the number of missed calls a day, comments and messages clearly showing their username, and anything personal they might have posted about you. Catch it before they delete it. It will be useful later.
- Change your passwords, switch your social media profiles to private (at least for now), get rid of any contact information like your phone numbers or emails anywhere you might still have them displayed.
- If you can, do a complete social media detox, and ask a friend you can trust to watch out for anything that might be posted about you, and take those screenshots for you. Sometimes, leaving the online sphere for a while will get rid of the troll (you ignoring them takes their fun away), but it will also clear your head and help you feel more grounded and present.
- When you're ready, gather your evidence and report it. Not only will this help you back into being in control, but it might also prevent the cyberbully from bothering other people.

Why Does Bullying Happen?

We have already briefly touched on some of the reasons behind bullying earlier, and from what I've gathered, people often find it helps to know a bit more about the big why. Of course everyone is different and no particular definition applies to all, but there are some patterns researchers have identified that tend to repeat themselves in people with bullying tendencies.

They've found that ridiculously, some bullies target other people just for entertainment (this is especially common in cyberbullying), or to get extra attention from their peers, when they feel like they aren't getting enough of it.

Others use bullying as a strategy to advance themselves at work, to feel like they have power over people, or bully people who have more potential or better skills to inaction or fear, so that they can bag a promotion instead of them. At college, they might steal your work and claim it as their own, or demand that you complete their projects for them. They use other people to create false progress and gains.

Some people turn to bullying because they've been feeling left out and unpopular. They then project their own frustrations onto their target, or use the person to try and join a closed group, and become more prominent. This is why it's quite a common scenario to see popular characters dominating the entire college or workplace without anyone daring to interfere or stand up to them.

There are also times when people bully others because they were previously victims of bullies themselves. If someone was bullied at school, they might think the best way to get back control is by bullying other people too. In their eyes, it's a way to become the ones in power and get revenge.

Then there's prejudice. That as a topic in itself would make for an entire series of books. And while the logic behind all reasons for bullying is twisted, prejudice against someone based on them being different in any way, shape or form, can of course never ever be justified.

Why Do Some People Stay Quiet?

People who are being bullied often stay quiet. But it's not like they don't want to say anything. In fact, they usually think about speaking up all the time. But in reality, it's tough. It's hard to even imagine being questioned about something so painful and personal.

Here are some common reasons why some people endure it silently:

- Feeling afraid things will get worse if the bully finds out they've told someone. Being worried that if the bully gets in trouble with HR, they might increase the intensity to get even.
- Feeling afraid people won't believe them, especially if the bullying only happens when nobody else is around.
- Feeling afraid that others will think of them as a snitch or a tattletale.

- Feeling embarrassed by the situation, and worried others will think they're weak.
- Worried that admitting they're being bullied will ruin their reputation at work or in a social group that matters to them.
- Hoping that if they put up with the bullying just for a day or two longer, they'll eventually be accepted into the group.
- Feeling shy and afraid of drawing even more attention to themselves by speaking up.
- Believing there's nothing they can do, and can't think of anyone else they know would have their back.
- Feeling cornered and being threatened into staying quiet.
- Thinking bullying is normal and they just have to put up with it (false!).

And Finally, What CAN We Do?

Finally, let's talk about how we can break this vicious cycle.

Bullies only keep coming back like clockwork to people they perceive as an easy target. To stop this from happening on a continuous basis, we need the kind of action that will break that easy peasy pattern for them. As soon as things start changing and getting difficult or unprecedented for the bully, they will most likely back off.

If you suspect that you, or anyone you know has been subject to bullying, there are things you can do, either together with a friend or alone, to remove yourself or your friend from the situation.

Keep Engagement To Bare Minimum

Bullies expect big reactions like crying, fear, swearing or fighting, and are encouraged by them. As a principle, engagement is encouragement. So whenever you can, keep your engagement and reactions to the bare minimum. Of course this is not always possible, so do defend yourself when you need to. But when you can, being ignored and seeing you undisturbed as you just keep on walking, will throw the bully off balance. They'll start feeling less sure of themselves.

Put your headphones on, count to ten, repeat to yourself you're strong and you can keep walking. Ignoring the bully will take away their power.

Here are some pointers to help you do this:

- Don't pay attention to the bully directly.
- Don't make eye contact with the bully at any point. Don't look back as you're walking away.

- Keep walking even if the bully follows you, and try to find a safe place, like a cafe, a busy shop, or approach the nearest group of people.
- Use confident body language (it works even when inside you don't feel like it). Square your shoulders, raise your head, and walk at a good resolute pace, like you have important places to be.
- If you feel like you're in danger, call someone while you're walking away. Focus on the person you're talking to and try to sound as casual as possible.
- Set up a code word with a few friends, use it and then give a clear hint where you are, so that they can find you.

If this is not possible or you're outnumbered, focus purely on self defense and finding your way out as quickly as possible. Avoid eye contact, or addressing them directly. Just get out.

Avoid The Bully As Much As Possible

To reduce the frequency of bumping into each other, predict your possible interactions, or places where they usually wait for you, and avoid them as much as you can.

- Walk with other people so the bully can't single you out. When your friends are not around, you can keep close to a random pedestrian or a group of people on your way to and from classes or work.
- Take a different route whenever possible. If you have more than one route option, keep switching them randomly.

- Change your routine regularly to make it more difficult for the bully to guess what you're doing and where they can find you.
- Keep your social media profiles private and block the bully's account to reduce their access to updates about you. If you can, stop posting updates about what you're doing on social media altogether. Just until the situation resolves.
- Remove any other connections you have, like being members of the same groups or liking the same pages.

Make sure you're not being too obvious with your avoidance strategy. If a bully realizes that you are doing everything you can to avoid them, knowing you're affected by them might spur them on. So it's best to be discreet and make it look like you're just making these changes on a whim.

Document What The Bully Is Doing

Whether they have started on you or on someone else, make sure to press the record button in your pocket to record what the bully is saying, or try to take a few pictures. Just make sure the bully doesn't notice it. This works whether you are being bullied online or in real life.

For cyberbullies, you can document everything by taking screenshots, saving messages, recording voice calls. Just make sure to document all of these things right away before the bully can delete any evidence.

Outside, you can point out the street cameras to the bully, making sure they know they're being recorded. If you don't manage to record or take pictures on your phone, write down everything that happened as soon as you can. Evidence always makes a huge difference, regardless of the type of action you decide to take next, or who you decide to talk to in the end.

Reach Out To Someone

Difficult as it might be, it's always a good idea to talk to someone about your situation. You don't have to go straight to the authorities, but talking to someone you trust is a great start. By reaching out to someone close to you, you can ease a lot of the stress and dread you are feeling each time the bully approaches you. The person you confide in might also have some good advice to offer. More importantly, you might be able to work together to overcome the problem.

Even if you are an adult and you're being bullied at work, this is something you can do to make things better. Who knows? You might even discover that the person you have decided to tell has experienced something similar in their previous life.

Never Try To Bully Back

Bullying back can escalate the situation faster than you can imagine. It's a direct form of engagement and participation in a toxic situation, and it's also the type of response bullies thrive on. They want to hear rude comments, they want you to expose yourself in a fight. If you respond and try to get them back, it will only make them want to step up their game, and turn the whole thing into a competition.

The more active or inventive your participation becomes, the harder it's going to be to eventually stop and head for the exit. Any of the evidence you might have gathered will no longer be a tool you can use to your advantage, because now there's likely to be evidence of you doing the same as well.

It's just not worth it. Trying to top their game will only drag you down to their level, and leave you even more exhausted in the long run. And that's something you definitely don't want to happen. Show the bully you know better!

Confront Them In A Way They Don't Expect

We've already established bullies expect the usual reactions, like crying, fear, or fights. However, there's another way you can react and confront them to catch them off their guard. And that's speaking up in a surprisingly frank way. Even though this might initially be hard to do, the results can be groundbreaking. Here's a few to try:

- Say "Stop!" or "Leave me alone!" in a loud and firm voice, with the impression of being absolutely calm. You can also say something like, "What you're doing isn't ok!" This will surprise them as most likely they're not expecting you to be quite so upfront. There's also a chance this will catch the attention of passers by, which is something the bully is scared of.
- Ask them why. Simply asking "Why are you doing this?" can be enough for them to be thrown out of

their zone, and then you can take advantage of the moment of surprise and get out of the situation. And don't get the bullies wrong—they are not all that tough. Chances are they'll ponder your question later on when they're alone.
- If you are a generally funny person, try saying something funny when the bully approaches you (without targeting them personally). This can reduce the tension and distract them, giving you the moment's advantage.

After saying your piece, walk away. If you're standing up for a friend, take their arm and walk away together. Do this even if the bully hasn't stopped talking.

In some cases, speaking up in this way can actually turn into an opportunity to connect and communicate with the bully. You might be the first person to ever stand up to them and by doing this, you will establish the notion you aren't in fact weak. Your bully might be ok to then chat with you, especially if it makes them look more interesting in their friend's eyes. They will start seeing you in a different light.

It's important to note that speaking up isn't the same as bullying back. By speaking up, you are sending a message that you won't just sit back and allow things to happen. Keep things brief and abstract though, and be wary it might be easy to re-trigger the bully if they take something you said personally. This is not the time to try teaching them a lesson, but rather to make them see the human side of you (and of themselves).

Show Compassion

No doubt—bullying is a horrible thing to do. But there can be times when the bully is lashing out because deep inside, they are also hurting. It might even be quite a while since someone has been nice to them. But this will take courage. It takes a lot of character and strength to show empathy to someone who's being horrible. But if you know you are a compassionate person at heart, don't let this amazing part of you go just because of a bully. Instead, use it to try and see through their mask.

And if they react positively, you can turn things around for both of you. If it doesn't work, then both of you will still take away the fact you were the bigger person in the situation.

Keep Your Spirit

Finally, try to maintain your true essence and some positivity throughout the experience. This can be super challenging, especially if negative emotions are skyrocketing and you feel like giving up. But don't. You can do this.

Keep in mind it's not your fault.

Be compassionate and kind to yourself, and stay patient with your feelings.

Never allow the bully to derail your life. Keep going and keep strong. Even if you are fighting silently, the important thing is that you are fighting. Things will change. You'll make them change.

You Aren't Alone

Now it's FINALLY time for some positive stories. I'm all about positive stories! (In case you couldn't tell).

Some of them might surprise you, but they are proof that virtually anyone can become a target regardless of their personality or background. They are also an inspiration showing us bullying can be stopped, and doesn't have to remain at the forefront of someone's life forever.

Personally, I was fascinated to hear about Jackie Chan. He's starred in like 130 movies and counting, with his roles nearly always embracing martial arts and fighting for justice, and him knocking over bad guy after bad guy like they're paper clowns. And yet, as he's shared many times by now, he used to be a target of bullies when he was young.

For a long time, he just put up with the bullying quietly because he was scared and didn't know how to defend himself at all. But when a new student joined his school and he witnessed the same thing being done to him, something inside Jackie bubbled up, and he jumped in to defend the new kid. By standing up, he found his courage, and realized he can in fact stand up for himself too. He described this as one of the key breakthrough moments of his young life.

Tough as Eminem might seem now, he has also opened up about being bullied a lot when he was young. They had to move often and he was changing schools all the time. Being the new kid is always tough. Bullies shoved him into lockers, waited for him in hallways and bathrooms. He said he could have allowed all these things to ruin his life, but later chose not to, and became determined to show people what he could do. And boy did he find his voice!

Selena Gomez has shared about her experience with cyberbullying. She is one of the most followed people on social media, but she actually hates using it. It's because she gets an extreme amount of personal negative comments and upsetting messages from trolls, and finds it incredibly hard not to feel anxious and hurt. Even though she also receives countless positive messages from her fans, she said she feels like each negative comment cuts through her soul ten times more. And they always keep coming. She has deleted all social apps from her phone countless times.

Yet she's also strong enough to make a point of finding a way to show the trolls her back and motivate herself to move forward. After all, she knows she needs to fight for those who believe in her, and more importantly, for herself.

Now, quite a few people were also shocked to discover that Elon Musk was once a victim of bullies too. Of course, the Elon Musk we know today is a confident and powerful business heavyweight, and a bit of an icon in the world of entrepreneurs (just a bit).

But when he was younger, he was the shy and clever type who couldn't do sports and had a tough time socially. He hated waking up each day and dreading the bullies. But later on he's learned to embrace the very things that made him different and vulnerable then, as strengths. After all, if it wasn't for being quiet and spending a lot of time learning, maybe he wouldn't be one of the most successful people in worldwide business today.

Another familiar face who has opened up about bullying is Eva Mendes. She shared she used to be bullied by another girl for being petite. For a long time, she struggled to tell others about it out of fear. She only found the courage to confront the situation and her bully after two years. But she did! And that moment has changed her life and the way she saw herself to the point she felt like she could literally do anything.

And that's just a few examples. Many more people who are doing great today used to once deal with bullying. At some point in their lives, they had been as scared, frustrated, and lost as you (or someone you know) might be feeling now. But instead of allowing the experience to ruin their lives, they found a way to overcome it.

So, you are not alone. Of course, every situation is different in essence, but just like them you have the strength to stand up and come out of this. You can do it! I believe in you. Can you believe in yourself too?

You are STRONG

Of course—right now, you might feel like you're not actually sure. What if you don't have the strength everyone keeps going on about? What if you are dreading the moment you'll meet the bully again because you always completely freeze? And that's totally ok. Really. I used to feel the same as well.

But the good thing is you don't have to be different, or behave like you're someone else for the rest of your life. All you need to do is find a way out of this. Once you're out, that's the job done.

Imagine the positive things that will happen then. The lightness, the ease of mind, the sense of freedom and the feeling of having overcome something that has been draining you for some time. You'll feel more yourself. You'll enjoy the things you love doing more, as there won't be any heaviness lurking at the back of your mind (or at least not of this kind).

This is YOUR life.

Even if you aren't yet exactly convinced, give it a chance. Don't do it for anyone else but for yourself, and the people in your life who love you. You can try a few things out, see what works for you and what doesn't.

Would you agree that your happiness deserves to be given a shot? And more than just one?

Good. Now, here is one more thing to remember:

Professional Help Does Help

It's in our nature to sometimes perceive the need to seek professional help as embarrassing. We don't want our friends to know, we think talking to a therapist would expose us to judgment and more unbearable vulnerability. We don't want a stranger to sit there and watch us cry.

And yet, as people who have gone through therapy would all agree, once you've done your first couple of sessions and gotten used to it, it doesn't actually feel like that at all.

Therapy helps people process their tough experiences in a healthy and progressive way, and come up with strategies that work personally for them, every single day. Talking to a professional who is also a completely neutral figure in the situation (and in your life) is powerful, because once you adjust to the new and unknown setting, you won't feel exposed but understood instead. You'll gain an active listener. Someone who is interested enough to provide constructive feedback and the kind of encouragement you need to hear to feel less alone and stronger.

Bullying therapy usually means focusing on immediate strategies and defence ideas you can start applying straight away in your real life. You'll also dive a bit deeper into the story or any background events or triggers that might be relevant to the situation, or might have contributed to the way things are now. A professional therapist will use well-researched and science-approved specific techniques and exercises to help you through the process. They'll use methods that gently and gradually offset the weight of the trauma and anxiety connected with bullying, which will shift your perspective and stir up your attention, so that you can stride forward. And most importantly, you'll start healing.

Still on the fence?

If facing a therapist one-on-one in an intimate environment such as their office seems just too much right now, there are other ways you can get similar benefits yet remain slightly more anonymous or laid back.

You can join a therapy group, or any set-up similar to the social enterprise group the girl I had an oat-milk cappuccino with earlier in the book attended, to help overcome her experience with bullies. A therapy group setting is amazing, because it takes some of the focus off your own experience and mind, and you get to hear about the things other people are going through, how they react, what they do to make themselves feel better, what they try to avoid. You become an active listener too, and could potentially play a part in the healing process of others, which can be a super powerful support tool for your own recovery in return.

You can buddy up with someone who's going through a similar experience or struggle. Then you can support each other, challenge each other, hold each other accountable. And you'll likely make a new awesome friend.

Lastly, if you can't find a suitable group in your area, you can always call a free bullying helpline to find someone with experience who will listen. They will be able to share some useful resources with you, explain some options available to you in more detail, recommend suitable counselling sessions, or point you out to the nearest help centre or support club.

Doesn't sound quite that bad now, does it?

The bottom line is, therapy can provide amazing support and guidance when you really need it. It can help you believe in yourself a bit more again. You'll learn some new things about yourself in the process. It can help you get yourself back on track.

> I don't know how my story will end, but nowhere in my bio will it ever say "I gave up".

Add your notes:

BREAK THE CYCLE

LAYING YOUR STEPPING STONES

Whew! That chapter was heavy (wipes forehead).

I'm so proud of you for sticking around! And I definitely feel like I need a little break. I'm off to make some fresh mint tea—if you feel similar, take as much time as you need as well.

On the next page is a mandala you can color if you want. Let's meet back here in fifteen!

All done?

Awesome. Let's continue. Now it's time to break some of the other cycles that may be keeping you running in endless circles.

As we've already talked about a bit earlier in this book (and in my previous book *Break Through The Noise* as well), learning how to create better self-confidence and healthier self-esteem includes recognizing negative patterns, accepting the fact that they are most probably your roadblocks, and then breaking through them. And just like any other effort you make in your life everyday, it's best to take things one step at a time. That way, you don't end up raising the bar so high that you can never realistically reach it. Instead, keeping things at a level that requires some work but at the same time is actually achievable, will see you progressing far more steadily.

That said, let's start with a bit of self-reflection. I know, it's becoming a bit of a theme now, isn't it? But that's because it really works, especially when it's done intentionally as a goal-specific exercise.

For starters, let's think about your values. Your personal principles that you cherish the most. Causes that are the closest to your heart. Missions that you'd like to one day accomplish to make your world, or the world, a better place.

This is important, because it reassures you about the things that truly matter to you. Even once you have built higher confidence, you won't always be in a position to influence or contribute to everything, so you'll have to pick your battles. And save your energy for the ones that are key to you.

So go ahead, write down your non-negotiables as they stand right now. When I've done this (and I've done this a lot more than once), I was actually quite surprised about some of mine. Yes, they might change, but seeing them in black and white as they stand now will build a pretty solid base for what comes next.

The Prep Work

In order to break those negative cycles in your life, you must start within. With your mindset. With your inner voice. With becoming self-reliant. Keep your mind open to the potential impact these changes really could have on the way you navigate your life. Even if, at times, they sound a little too... you know... self-helpy. It's all part of it. The skeptics might suggest otherwise. But, the only way you can find out if it works for you and your mind, is to give it a genuine try.

And to give yourself the chance to be impressed with your own work. Because acceptance, validation, and appreciation are always the most profound when they first come from you.

Now that you have written down your values, it's time to get started. In a nutshell, here's the ground we will be covering here:

- All about self-respect and self-acceptance
- How to navigate a mindset shift towards positivity
- Transforming your inner voice into a friendly one
- How to set yourself some low-key but effective challenges
- How to keep track and make sense of your work

In this chapter, we'll define each of these points in more detail. As you work through each of them, you'll likely feel at least a little shift with every step. Just remember to work at your own pace so that you can actually meet the expectations you set for yourself. This, in turn, will keep you motivated all the way down to breaking that finish line ribbon! Let's go.

Set Your Boundaries

Psychologically speaking, boundaries are the relational, spiritual, emotional, and mental limitations on which external influences you are or aren't willing to accept.

Practically speaking, your personal boundaries are a big part of self-respect and self-acceptance. Recognizing and setting your boundaries means being mindful of how a situation makes you feel, and communicating clearly with yourself and with others whether you're comfortable, whether or not you agree, and in which direction you see yourself going without upsetting your personal preferences or your values. It means respecting your space and your bubble, and finding the right balance between compromise and your own feelings and opinions.

When you aren't clear on where you think your boundaries should be and tend to struggle with setting them, you probably get overwhelmed easily as other people invade your personal space. As this happens, you tend to just accept things that are happening instead of effectively asserting the situation yourself or making your own decisions.

If you have been dealing with low confidence or a compromised self-esteem, setting clear boundaries might seem like a challenging thing to do right now. It might be hard to imagine where to start, or know how to tell others what you actually think. And yes, it can be daunting at first, especially when you've usually let others take the lead. But it's important that you do it. Your voice is a voice, and it matters, even if it maybe doesn't sound super confident at first. To help you out, remember this:

- You don't have to compromise your values so that others accept you. In fact, real friends will always remember and respect your preferences, wishes or triggers, no matter what. Just voice them more clearly and explain how important they really are to you.
- Don't accept anything you don't feel comfortable with.
- Be aware of your non-negotiables and remember you don't have to compromise on them.
- If you feel strongly against something, let the other person know. If they don't listen or are super keen to

make you change your mind to benefit their own agenda, walk away.
- You have the right to be who you want to be, and to express yourself in whichever way makes you feel happy and comfy in your skin.
- People will not always agree with you and that's cool, they really don't have to. As long as you know you've done the best for yourself and your conscience, you are good.

All that said, make sure to find a balance between staying in your comfort zone and challenging it. Don't let your boundaries become walls. They need to stay on the healthy side. Sometimes we take things to the other extreme and restrict ourselves too much. So always make sure to listen to the friends and family members you trust. We need to be open to other people's perspectives and consider them, to keep our personal bubbles objective and healthy.

Keep your gut feeling alert and on the forefront, but when it comes to genuine people you trust and people you have good chemistry with, allow yourself to be consciously free, independent, and open.

Say No When No Feels Right

Another extremely important step to take to break the cycle of things that might be holding you back, is to stop trying to please other people. Difficult as it might be sometimes, saying no to others when it feels right to you, is also a part of setting healthy boundaries.

One of my friends is actually a people pleaser (he's working on it), and people do see him as too dependable sometimes. He has a tendency to say yes to everything. I mean, every bit of extra work, every request, every night out, even when inside he doesn't really want to do it at all. And I've seen people try to walk over him sometimes, to benefit themselves. Needless to say that when this happens, it's not doing anything positive for his self-confidence whatsoever.

That's why finding the assertiveness to say no when it matters is super important. I've been helping my friend to work through this the best I can, and it is a process, but I also know that every time he does stand up for himself and his feelings, it is a small victory that leaves him buzzing. So it's worth it.

Give yourself the permission to think about things first, see how they fit into your schedule, eliminate the risk of burnout if you're having too much on your plate, or just take a bit more time before you answer if you aren't sure how you feel about something. And if you are not feeling it, just say no. It will become easier over time.

Speak Up As Needed

Of course, staying silent and going with the flow is often easier. But it also sucks when it causes a conflict within yourself because it feels like giving in.

When you don't speak up, people won't know what you want, how you feel, and who you are. You don't have to be confrontational or sharp. Just expressive enough to get the message across. If you are working on a group project and are highly suspicious the others are dumping most of the hardest work on you, speak up. If a friend is always asking you for favors but then is hesitant to return even just one of those favors, speak up. Or if someone is talking to you harshly, speak up.

It's time to break the silence. As you learn how to speak up for yourself more often, the confident person inside you will build the courage to come out too.

Spotlight On Positivity

Are you a generally positive person?

Surprisingly (or maybe not), many people struggle with answering this question honestly. Sure, we all want to say we are positive. But on the inside, for many people the actual truth is that being a positive person at heart is only someone they aspire to be.

Do you relate to this?

That's ok, because positivity is a funny one anyway. Sometimes we can't even be sure how to define it. Does positivity mean we force ourselves to always say we are ok, even when we really aren't? Does it mean we should wear pink glasses to trick ourselves into seeing something that isn't true? Does positivity mean we shouldn't see our problems for what they are, or even ignore them altogether?

No.

Here, we'll approach positivity differently. One thing we won't do is use false positivity to keep our heads in the clouds. Instead, we will learn to look at reality in two ways.

This simply means that whenever a challenging situation comes up, you'll first look at it objectively, the way it really is, and learn to observe and admit the facts. Even if they are grim. You just absorb them, analyze what they mean.

And after that, you ask yourself: What realistic steps can I take to change this situation for the better? How can I stir things to take a new, more likeable direction?

That's where the positivity mindset comes in. To me, being a positive person means you're able to remain realistic but also build a habit of always looking for ways things could change for the better. And wear the pink glasses just for fun.

This, in turn, empowers you to also start believing in your own abilities and strengths. When you do come up with some steps and start taking action, you're stirring things up. You are changing direction. And when things work out for the better, your overall confidence and trust in your own judgment will flourish. Soon, focusing on the positive twist will become your new amazing habit.

Of course, things won't always go well or work out the way you wanted them to, but that's all part of the game. The important thing is that you've tried and at least learned something. Often, the "failure" to change things the way you thought you could, opens a completely different perspective, or a glimpse of a path you couldn't see before at all.

Now, let's explore some ways that can help ease you into creating the habit of a more flexible mindset, one that is open to the possibility of creating your own positive options:

Look After Your Headspace

Mindfulness is a great tool you can use to monitor your feelings and learn to gain control over some of your reactions.

Reactions and feelings are not always so closely intertwined —you can feel about something strongly and yet learn to keep awareness of your rational mind to help you react in a way you won't regret later.

First, always remind yourself to accept your true feelings without judgment or without thinking they're stupid. Because they definitely aren't. Then, when you feel a strong reaction coming, accept the feeling of emotion first, if need be, just for that moment, in a "I'll deal with you later" kind of way. Then, try to focus on your rational mind, and how you'd probably react to the situation if you were calm. This won't come naturally at first, but it's definitely possible to do.

To help you get used to being mindful, you can try techniques like focusing on your breathing, guided meditation podcasts or audiobooks, taking a pause every day to just let yourself think, and focusing on one feeling, task, or problem at the time. These techniques will help strengthen your mind, reduce some stress, and promote your overall mental wellbeing, as well as help you look for those famous positive twists.

The reason mindfulness can be so helpful is that it makes you slow down and you don't feel too rushed or overwhelmed all the time. It helps you monitor how you feel, and recognize which reactions and actions you take under pressure make you feel better than others when you think about them afterwards.

Keep practicing at your own comfortable pace, and soon you'll notice you've become just generally more... aware. And possibly calmer. Fantastic work!

Prioritize Self-Care

Whenever you don't feel at your best physically, it can be super hard to motivate yourself mentally and emotionally. It doesn't exactly add to feeling confident either. But stepping up your everyday self-care game can be easy, and you'll end up more energized.

For me, it always helps to remind myself how hard my body works every day to keep me alive. There's so much going on all the time. And yet I'm not even consciously aware of most of the things my body does. So the least I can do is show that I care as well.

To keep it easy, you can focus on the things that might seem basic but make a huge difference on the daily. Like getting enough sleep each night, making sure you sleep enough that you actually wake up refreshed and not still tired. Getting some exercise. Spending some time outside every day. Eating more whole foods instead of heavily processed stuff, at least a few times a week (you don't have to deprive yourself of the things you like eating, just add more healthy stuff as and when you can).

Of course, looking after your mind plays a huge part in self-care as well. So make sure you free-up some time to do the things you truly love doing, and things that make you feel great. When you look after your physical and mental health equally well, it becomes easier to deal with everyday challenges, as well as sweating the bigger stuff.

Be Kind To Yourself First

Self-kindness is essential for increasing your overall vibe. Of course, we often have the tendency to doubt ourselves or put ourselves down when we make a mistake or do something wrong. But if this evolves into a pattern and becomes the way you feel most of the time, it can be really toxic.

Even more annoyingly, when we are so busy being disappointed with failures, we often don't see that they might have not actually been failures at all. We miss the opportunity to learn something, or to walk through a slightly different open door. I can't even count how many times this has happened to me.

To change this pattern, here are a few things to try for starters:

- Ask yourself: What would you say to your best friend, if this exact same situation happened to them? Chances are you wouldn't say that your friend is useless or a loser for making a mistake. So don't say it to yourself either. Instead, treat yourself and talk to yourself the same way you would to your best friend. Try to find the same positive twists to the situation you would try to find for them.
- Keep mindful of the things you're great at. Always remind yourself of your strengths, and of all the things that make you stand out.
- Allow yourself to feel out your emotions, both good and bad. Don't restrict yourself when you're excited or happy, and feel things out when you're sad or frustrated. Suppressing negative emotions will only result in them exploding even more uncontrollably later.
- Try to turn around any unproductively self-doubtful

thoughts. For example, when you notice you're thinking "I always get in trouble because I am always late," you can transform this to "I am always late so I need to start planning my schedule." Now you have twisted a negative thought into a more productive one which signals potential to change things for the better. Instead of feeling bad about always being late, you have a new action point on your to-do list.
- Never, and I mean never, compare yourself to other people. You are unique. You are your own person. Always remember that your situation and circumstances differ from those of others. So, it isn't fair for you to compare yourself to someone else, especially if it makes you feel bad or inadequate. Because you aren't bad or inadequate. You're just different. And that's a good thing.

Next, it's time to branch out. Make a small effort to find and focus on some positive twists every day. You could sit down with your favourite drink, or with your dog, and write down all the things you appreciate about yourself (if it seems hard, start with the things the dog appreciates about you! That should get you in the spirit of it nicely). Then, keep the list safe and refer to it often.

Or, you could start agreeing more with the compliments other people give you. Most of us often tend to wave compliments off like flies, without realizing that actually, they have a point.

Challenge yourself every now and then. The comfort zone has its place and it's where you recharge, but stepping out of it is super powerful, especially if you are struggling to find motivation or goals. You can buddy up with a friend who will hold you accountable and motivate you through the challenges you set up for yourself. For me as a writer, getting out and moving my body more has always been a struggle, but it helped a lot when my friend and I agreed we would send each other photos of being out in the park wearing our running trainers every single morning. And yeah, neither one of us wants to be the one who loses!

And of course, always celebrate every win. Create a brand new pattern, one that focuses on kindness, actionable takeaways and more brightness, and when you do, other good things will fall in place. And remember:

You're taking a stand by choosing to help yourself.

Why So Many People Love Gratitude Journals

Yep, you've probably heard about keeping this thing called a gratitude journal before. Literally everyone and their mom has been recommending writing gratitudes. To be completely honest, I kept hearing about it so much it was tiring, and I first decided to try it just to prove (not sure to whom) it was all just a fad.

Apparently, the best time of day for writing gratitudes was supposed to be first thing in the morning, right after you wake up. So I set up a new notepad and a pen on my bedside table, and started the next few mornings with writing the things I was grateful for, still half asleep in bed.

The funny thing about writing something as soon as you wake up, is that you're in a haze. Your conscious mind is only about half awake and the rest of you is still running on subconscious. You might still have one foot in your dream, and can just barely separate the reality from it. So get ready—some of the stuff you write in that state will be hilarious. And when you're done, after you've walked over to the kitchen and made some coffee, I guarantee you won't remember a thing you actually wrote down.

So I learned to come back to read my gratitudes whenever I had a minute later in the day. And I was so surprised by what I read and how it actually made me feel.

Some of my gratitudes were funny, just relating to stuff I dreamt about, or made very little sense. Others though, were heartwarming and so profound in their simplicity.

Pointing out things I'd never normally think twice about, like:

- *I'm so grateful I have this warm and safe bed to sleep in.*

- *I appreciate my body for waking me up, and functioning. How does it even do it?*
- *This new day just got real and I can't wait to go out walking first thing.*
- *I'm grateful for inspirational people who put themselves out there to help others in any big or small way.*
- *I love waking up and hearing the cats play as they welcome the day.*
- *I appreciate all the work and writing I've done, and all the work and writing I have yet to do.*
- *I'm grateful that I'm breathing and I'm not in any pain.*

This is not even a joke, I thought. I wrote that. This stuff is real af.

Just... my own mind kept surprising me. Some time ago for example, I used to suffer with my teeth a lot, and while saving up to have two of them removed and replaced with implants, I spent countless days wondering what living without physical pain, or without being loaded on painkillers, used to feel like. And now, writing that down wasn't me being clever or rational. That was my subconscious talking. I was actually grateful for the things my rational mind already took for granted again. And yeah, reading back these gratitudes always made an impact on the rest of my day.

I never expected that.

So, if you have been feeling quite sceptical like me, consider giving it a try. Just to see not if, but how much you can surprise yourself!

Personalize It

This exercise is all about you and your words. So it doesn't matter whether you want to pick up a nice hardcover journal for your gratitudes to make things a bit more official, or whether you just want to keep it easy and put a bunch of loose papers and a pen by your bed. It's totally up to your own preference. Your words are the most important part of this.

You can also write exactly how you like to. Write it as a story, or just write in bullet points. After a while, I began to skip the "I'm grateful for" phrase, and just wrote in short one-liners. Sometimes I did drawings instead. Anything works.

Also, if you absolutely can't imagine writing anything first thing as you wake up, you could do this in the evenings just before you doze off. This could be an amazing exercise to help you relax if you normally have trouble falling asleep. And the next day, you'll be just as surprised to read what you wrote the night before. The key thing is to try and make it part of your daily routine for about a week, and then see where it goes, and whether you want to keep it up.

Don't think about what you think you should write, or what you think you should be grateful for. Instead, just let your mind and your thoughts flow, and write honestly. I've most definitely written things like "the new vitamin c face cream", or "the way we laughed together at the bar last night". If you feel it, then it's real, and it's worth the note.

This approach to gratitude journaling really gives you the chance to experience self-reflection that's honest and genuine in existence. Even if you have to be half asleep to discover it. It's an amazing way to feel the connection you have with your super unique (and super mysterious) subconscious mind.

Train Your Inner Voice To Be Nicer

Whenever something bad happens, have you noticed the little voice in your head which seems to take this obscene pleasure in making things worse?

For example, if you're presenting something important in a meeting and you get a blackout, that little voice immediately comes alive and says, "You should have practiced more!", even though you know that in actual reality, you spent hours on this. Or, if you have studied so hard for an exam and you still don't get a passing grade, that little voice will be so quick to say, "See, that's because you took those breaks to get actual sleep!"

I once had a friend who I thought was my best friend sometimes, but I could never be sure because she liked to switch her preferences. Like, a lot. Almost every week it felt like she was choosing one of the others to hang out with instead, and I always had to compete for her attention. As you can imagine, every time she chose someone else over me, my inner voice went mad. It made me think I wasn't a good friend to her. It made me feel like I wasn't eligible, and she was just making whatever choice was best for her, followed by the inevitable "I told you so". Like there was something wrong with *me*.

I don't actually think there's a single person on this planet who doesn't have to deal with a negative inner voice at least sometimes.

And while this voice often seems to have a persistent life of its own, it is actually possible to control it. You can definitely learn how to become the one calling the shots. You can be the one who in the end says enough is enough. If a real person was saying those things to you, you wouldn't stand for it either. So, don't ever accept them as facts.

And, wanna know what's even better? You can train that voice to become nice.

Catch It Out And Prove It Wrong

Start out by catching the nagging voice in the act as often as you can. Next time something goes wrong, like a project being so unexpectedly hard that you missed a deadline, and the first thing that goes through your head is "That's because you're not the right person for this job," notice it straight away. Catch it and pinpoint it. Then, challenge it. Because deep inside, you actually know the real reason you didn't meet the deadline. It was because of something unexpected, and not because of you being inadequate. So, don't tolerate it.

Instead, prove it wrong.

After recognizing a destructive thought, implement the positive twist exercise from earlier, and try to look for ways to make missing that deadline less impactful. Put together a quick excerpt of the work you did complete, containing the parts you know your boss needs the most, to give them at least some data to go by. If you've tried to be too detailed and that's why the project took you so long, learn from this and next time focus on the most important bullet points first. Talk to your boss honestly about what happened.

And remember, everyone makes hiccups happen, even people who've been in their job for years. It just happens. So no, it's not because you can't do it. That thought was too harsh. So don't give it any more screen time. Just swipe left.

Of course there will be times when you can't fix things and that's ok. It happens too. But you can always tell yourself that you will try harder next time, you know now what not to do, and at least you've learned something from it. Keep offsetting those negative thoughts with consciously positive thoughts that are aimed at action taking and staying compassionate with yourself.

This means keeping your expectations realistic. Remember to keep the bar at the height where it's actually possible for you to jump over it. This in turn gives the negative voice far fewer opportunities to have a go.

Stop It From Stopping Your Future

Once you get better at noticing and calling out the negative voice whenever it's being unfair about something that has already happened, another step you can learn is preempting and transforming this voice when it tries to stop you from doing something in the future.

Listening to the negatives as they are trying to grow roots in your mind could make you miss out on life opportunities, new important relationships or just on doing something fun. Because these doubts and worries are making you freeze and then turn around and walk away from the possibility. And by doing that, they could potentially be stopping you from both personal or professional growth.

For many people, this happens far too often.

Like when you get invited to a dinner party. This dinner party has great potential for networking or making friends, because loads of people from your industry or people passionate about similar interests will be there. But you are feeling too self-conscious or anxious, and doubting whether you should go at all.

These people will notice you're nervous, your inner critic starts. You don't know as much as them about the topic. You know you struggle to make yourself heard in front of strangers. It will be a disaster. You don't have the confidence. And just like that, these doubts eventually drive you a little crazy and talk you into staying home.

Stop.

Take a deep breath. Acknowledge the negative doubts and thoughts for what they really are. They're just horror scenarios, products of your imagination, with no actual guarantee behind them. This means you can transform them completely.

Turn them into something realistically positive, like:

These people don't really know you, so how could they know what you look like when you're nervous? And of course there will be people with various levels of knowledge, so chances are you won't be the one who knows the least. And even if you are, at least you'll hear about something new. Aim for the smallest of commitments. Promise yourself you'll go for an hour, and if you feel too uncomfortable or things are awkward and don't improve, you'll go home. The odds are high that won't happen. You'll probably enjoy yourself in the end, and make some new meaningful connections.

Doing this will take a lot of effort and awareness. But just like any other skill, transforming your inner critic becomes easier the more you practice. Just keep noticing those thoughts, stop them when they come out, and consciously change them into something that will motivate, inspire, and make you feel curious.

Fight your inner critic by giving yourself enough chances to explore your possibilities. Even if you do end up going for just an hour.

Emotions Are Part Of The Deal

Although you might sometimes (or often) feel bothered by your emotions, they don't do that purposely. They exist to convey messages. You just have to learn how to read those messages when you can, and interpret them correctly.

Part of changing your inner voice is learning to translate and manage your emotions too. I'm not talking about controlling your emotions because of what other people might say. I want you to do it for you. For example, if you're someone who tends to give in to anger often, the toxic negative inner voice is probably poisoning you a great deal too. Or if you allow your moods to swing you sidewards too much, you might feel unstable, not really knowing what to expect from your mind, not just tomorrow, but even an hour from now.

However, this doesn't mean that you shouldn't allow yourself to feel anything either. Repressing your emotions is just as harmful as allowing them to take complete control.

Instead, stay somewhere in the middle.

Accept your emotions as part of the deal. Part of life. Name them, and whenever you can, try to understand where they're coming from and why. This will help you bring conscious awareness about your feelings, and stay at least somewhat in control, while not sweeping them under the carpet altogether.

And always remember that every emotion, positive or negative, always changes in the end. So will this anger. So will this sadness. It will evolve, fade, transform into a different feeling. Eventually. Always.

Notice things that help you calm yourself down, remember them, and use them next time to help yourself regain focus. Turn off your inner voice when it tries to make things worse or trigger you further. Just ignore it. Think of yourself like you would think of your best friend. You deserve the exact same compassion and understanding.

Sure, you need to stay accountable for your actions, and address consequences accordingly whether positive or negative, but never ever tell yourself off for *feeling*. That's just not even an option.

You don't need to give yourself more tough love. Life does enough of that already.

Map Your Mind

Have you heard of mind mapping before?

Mind mapping is a simple yet highly effective technique allowing you to organize your assumptions, thoughts, ideas, worries, wants and expectations visually.

A mind map is basically a framework you can use to explore things more thoroughly. You examine how connected your thoughts are to each other and how they affect each other. While people often use mind maps to plan creative projects, you can use yours as a self-reflection tool as well. It can help you see more clearly how your thought process works, recognize patterns, catch ideas or those little sparks of positivity and appreciation that might otherwise go unnoticed.

If you often feel easily overwhelmed by your mind, or if your thoughts and ideas seem to just be running around in chaos, a good mind map can be super beneficial in helping you to pull everything together and gain some clarity.

And although it sounds quite complex and possibly (just slightly) intimidating to be deconstructing your entire thought process on paper, it can actually be quite simple and fun. Many people report they enjoy this technique a lot, and use it all the time to clarify themselves on different ideas and life challenges. Here's how it works:

- Set a clear purpose and an objective for your mind map. If you're using it to get to the bottom of why you're struggling to feel more confident and resist peer pressure, your objective could be having a clearer picture of the feelings and fears that manifest themselves whenever someone challenges you. Later, you can use that information to plan what you're going to say next time it happens.
- If you'd like to break down and analyze multiple areas of your life or multiple challenges, create a

separate mind map with a separate objective for each of them.
- Make sure your mindset is right. You want to feel open-minded and calm enough to be 100% honest and fair to yourself in your reflections.
- When you're ready, start drawing your mind map. Begin from the central concept, which is the main challenge you've built your main objective on. Take the central challenge or question and write it in a box in the middle of your page.
- Around this central concept, write down your primary associations. These could be the first questions or issues that come to your mind, which contribute, influence, or are connected to your central challenge the most.
- Then, connecting to the first associations, write down your secondary associations, which could be any strengths or weaknesses you might have that contribute, influence, or are connected to your primary associations.
- Then, keep going with additional layers of associations until you feel like you've exhausted the central concept, or your mind, or the paper. The more associations you can connect and include, the better.
- Don't forget to draw clear lines to connect the associations exactly as they feed into one another, and number them, or use speech bubbles.
- For even more clarity, color-code your different layers, add drawings or charts. Make it yours.

BEFRIEND A MILLION MIRRORS

～⚭～

YOU, YOUR BODY, AND YOUR SELF

I'm so excited about this chapter!

Body positivity and self acceptance are yet another essential part of building up your self-esteem and confidence.

Sure, the way you see yourself and your body is always changing and will continue to change as you go through life, but the one crucial thing that remains the same and equally important at all times, is love.

Learning to love yourself as you are. Learning to like the person you see in the mirror. Learning to respect and appreciate your body.

Which can be quite a mission sometimes. I know. I'm definitely not all the way there either, and it's actually quite rare for someone to love everything about themselves all the time. So it's fine to just be somewhere on the spectrum, preferably remaining on the side of body positivity, love and acceptance as much as you can.

But the most important thing is to always aim to get as close to that respectful and compassionate point as possible. Even if sometimes you have to work hard and fight for it. Just make friends with the mirror. The results are so worth it.

Your Self Image

Knowing how to foster a positive and respectful self image is super important. The hard reality is, a lot of people struggle to keep up. There's so much pressure, so many versions of perceived perfection. So many ideas about the way we should look, dress, feel and behave, so many areas of life where we are expected to fit certain stereotypes.

But what if we don't fit them, or don't want to fit them?

The good news is, there's no such thing as total perfection, and no lifelong rule or requirement to follow any norms when it comes to looks, style, body shape, personal preferences, or love life.

The only valid measurement is how you feel the most yourself.

The other is your mindset—always working on the ability to love who you are, and feeling respectful and compassionate about your body.

Discovering your style and embracing things or changes that might make you feel better and more in your own skin are all part of it, given that they truly make you feel enhanced and you're not doing it for somebody else.

However, for these things to remain healthy and true to your real essence, you need to start from the core. Learn to love and respect your core. Not necessarily just for what it looks like, but mainly for what it represents. For all the hard work it does every day. For *who* it embodies.

For you.

Your body has been your home. Your only home. So you need to stay on good terms. You need each other. And when you learn to recognize this connection consciously every day, and appreciate yourself for who you are as a whole, beautiful, present, unique, vibrant human being, your confidence will start to grow strong roots.

Here are some suggestions to get you started:

- Shift your focus towards caring for your body the right way first. Do this by eating good nourishing food a few times a week, getting enough rest, spending time outside or doing something you love on the reg. Eating proper food often, instead of junk, lightens your body's workload.
- Don't force yourself to continue with something if you're feeling on the verge of burnout. Often check in with your body, and the way it feels physically. If you're exhausted, have a nap as soon as you can. If your brain is cloudy after a day of laptop work and you feel like running out of your apartment and not

stopping until you feel alive again, do it. Always assess your sources of energy. Have you been living on pot noodles and redbull for just a bit too long?
- Always look after your headspace. Once you've found a few mindful exercises that work for you, make sure you always have ten minutes to do them. Caring for yourself from within through mindfulness will improve your body's overall physical wellbeing as well.
- Think about how important your body truly is. Every single little part of it has a task, a purpose, or an amazing life-giving function. It needs your support, both emotionally and physically.
- Turn criticism into love. If you have a particular area of your body you feel unsure or frustrated about, and usually tend to criticize it in your mind, try to change the way you think about it. Right now, this is the part of you that literally needs the most love.
- When you catch a glimpse of yourself in the mirror, try to nurture positive thoughts. If I catch myself thinking something negative like my hair is a mess, I remind myself that in reality, I'm actually glad and grateful to even have this hair. I did the same when I used to think my nose was too big, or my shoulders too bony. While this of course will be of different significance to different people, making a conscious habit of turning criticism or negative remarks into realistic positivity always has an uplifting effect.
- Find as much inspiration in other people as you want, but without comparing yourself to them.

Inspiration is a booster, while comparison can often be quite toxic. There's always going to be someone who has something you don't, whether it's in personality, confidence, style, or features. Let yourself be inspired by the things you can influence. And as for the rest of it, think about how you can rock your own unique features. Noone else has them. And someone out there is definitely thinking they're beautiful. Own them. They're amazing.

- Always keep this at the back of your mind: If you would never say something about a friend's body, don't say it about your own either. Think about saying something nice instead, the same way you would want to say something nice to compliment a friend. It works!

Knowing Yourself

However, the way we look is only a small part of a much bigger picture. And so, we shouldn't allow ourselves to be totally defined by it. In fact, what's much more important for feeling in sync with your overall self, is working on knowing yourself, knowing your body, knowing its strengths and everything it is capable of, and the beauty of it that goes far beyond shape.

If you lose your awareness of that, it could impact the way you feel, and your self-esteem, on a whole new level that isn't nice at all. The last time this happened to me and I lost track, it took me a fair while to get over.

It was late spring, and I caught Lyme, which is a parasite you can get through a bite from an infected tick or a mosquito. Once it gets into your bloodstream and body, it basically feeds on your bones as it multiplies, and is quite tricky to get rid of. They say once you get Lyme, a trace of it will always remain in your blood.

Anyway, when my physician set the diagnosis she was also quite impressed, as a couple of blood tests showed my body was fighting the parasite super well. The number of my defensive white blood cells tripled. She said my body was holding up and full of strength.

Still, I needed to take a long course of antibiotics, which I generally don't get on with at all. They always make me nauseous, my stomach gets irritable and feels raw like it's lined with sandpaper. I usually lose a lot of appetite, even for foods I normally love. So, everything combined, I lost quite a bit of weight. However, the pills were helping, and in the end the Lyme was gone.

At first, I didn't care about the weight loss at all. I was just grateful to my body for being so strong, and for fighting the sucker off. Soon I started to feel like myself again, more substantial, ready to take my life back where I left off.

But I wasn't ready for what was lurking around the corner.

People's comments.

Granted, not everyone knew that I'd been ill. But still. The first few times, I just waved them off. But the more remarks I heard, the more self-conscious I became. Usually it went something like this:

Being so thin doesn't look healthy. You're too skinny. Go and have a burger. I don't eat animals, thank you. See? That's why you're so thin. No it's not. You don't know the first thing about my life. And on and on it went.

It was getting more and more difficult to brush these comments off. Suddenly, I forgot all about the good outcome. Instead of keeping in mind what a winner my body truly was, I started covering my bony shoulders no matter how hot the sun was. I let the negative comments creep into my consciousness and seed doubts.

Soon, I was giving more significance to appearance than substance. It was unfair. I'd been investing in my health and had much healthier habits than the people who were criticizing me, yet now they were winning. I felt hurt and trapped. I also lost it and overreacted a few times, then felt horrible about it after. I should have known better. I should know how to keep my emotions at bay.

An endless toxic cycle.

I knew something had to change. To come out of it, I had to choose myself over them.

It wasn't easy but I took a moment to analyze myself and how I had been dealing with the situation. I thought about how my body fought tirelessly to defeat the Lyme, to stay strong and on top of things. Then I thought about how, despite my body being so awesome and powerful, I couldn't even appreciate that anymore.

That's when the penny dropped, and I started working to bring myself back. I used my morning gratitudes to see what I appreciated about my body and my core. I continued to focus on my healthy eating, which I really loved by the way, and every day I reminded myself that these people really have no idea about my actual life, and it doesn't matter what they think about me.

Not anymore.

What really mattered was support, nourishment, appreciation, encouragement. I realized that sometimes you just can't get it all from others, and that's ok, because it should always come from you first anyway.

So… find the things you think are beautiful and impressive about your body and your whole being, and keep them close to your heart. Remind yourself how precious they are. Think about the assumptions you have about yourself and keep them straightforward and fair. Keep them real. Give your body and yourself credit for all the work, creativity, presence, beauty, authenticity, strength, sensitivity, love, the needs you have, the preferences you have, and the power you have to accept and embrace them.

Don't ever let anyone sidetrack you from knowing your strengths and knowing yourself.

Your Internal Dictionary

This goes hand in hand with training your inner voice to be nicer. This time, it's about the internal dictionary you use to describe yourself, your style, and the way you see yourself as a human being.

It's the words you use and the thoughts you have, when creating your own mental picture or personal view of yourself. This includes your whole core, your character traits, likes and dislikes, and appearance. It's how you see yourself in relation to the external world.

Have you ever thought about how you talk about yourself to others?

Let's find out. Think about the last time you introduced yourself to a new student, teammate at work, or when you described yourself at a job interview. What do you usually say when talking about your life having just met someone new? Be honest. Write them down if you can. Don't leave anything out, whether good or bad.

When you're done, compare the positive aspects of the way you see yourself with the negatives. When doing this exercise, many people will see more criticism in their own words than positivity. It's because we often find it easier to criticize or focus on what we think needs improvement. It's partly human nature and partly the way we're brought up. Many of us tend to see talking about ourselves positively as bragging. We will do it if the situation forces us, like in a job interview, but deep inside many of us can feel like it's inappropriate to talk about what we're good at.

It isn't.

Not if you're able to think about it objectively. Of course, when some people are overly confident, full of themselves and flash, it's annoying. But you aren't going to be like that. You're just going to keep a healthy balance, and be fair with yourself about your skills and your achievements. It is totally ok to talk about your successes, and to openly feel good about the things you like about yourself in front of others. It really is.

To put this in practice, try to challenge your self-criticism. Challenge each of the negatives you may have written individually one by one. Ask yourself honestly if it's really true. You might find many of them aren't. And even if some of them are, it can still be a good thing, because now you've separated the real ones from the ones you only projected on yourself. You have a more realistic picture, and you have something to work with. You can set up some goals that will help you challenge the negatives and work on them.

That way, you can eventually turn them into positives. Speaking of which, pay equal attention to the things you've included as likes. They matter just as much, if not more. Keep the list of likes, and refer back to it whenever you need a little pick-me-up. Add to it. All the time.

Challenging your self-criticism is one of the most effective ways to transform your self image and your internal dictionary into a more positive one. Don't forget to see the bigger picture, focus as much on the inside as you do on the outside. Keep doing this until you start truly believing how amazing you are. You have evidence of it now, after all. Stay real with it, and your self-esteem and confidence will start to grow healthily, but without becoming overbearing.

Mirroring

Looking in the mirror isn't always a walk in the park. Have you heard the story of the man who found looking at his reflection so challenging that he had to remove all the mirrors from his home?

It's true. Whenever he looked in the mirror, he always felt super strongly that he didn't like the person he saw in it. It was an everyday struggle. Although his friends insisted there wasn't anything wrong with him and complimented him all the time, he just couldn't see what other people saw. He put up with it for a while. But when it got so bad that he couldn't even check how he looked before leaving the house without feeling instantly put down, he decided to just throw them all away.

So he took down all the mirrors in his apartment, from the bedroom to the hallway to the bathroom, and donated them to his local thrift store.

It was an extreme solution that worked at first, and he felt liberated. However, after some time he realized that nothing had changed about his overall confidence. He was still feeling the same self-doubt. With or without the mirrors, his insecurities stayed where they were. He couldn't just donate those to the thrift store. He realized getting rid of the mirrors wasn't a sustainable solution (literally and figuratively). Plus, now he was even more worried about his actual appearance, because there was no way for him to check things before walking out the door.

His reflection wasn't the problem. So it was time to address the insecurities that were making him uncomfortable, and start working on his self-esteem from within. I bet he must be much better now because he decided to work on himself instead of just his surroundings.

At the same time, one thing stays clear—there is nothing wrong with wanting to look different if that's how you genuinely feel. Just try not to make any drastic changes out of desperation or frustration. Give yourself time to chew on the idea, taste it, experience a milder version of it first, to see how you could potentially really feel. Make sure you are sure. Patience is often so boring, and sometimes it even hurts to stay where you are for a while, but it is always worth the reassurance, the ripening of the idea, the personal growth that comes with it. And never try to change yourself for someone else, or to be like someone you're comparing yourself to, or competing with.

Always do it for yourself.

Also, remind yourself to think beyond your body's physical appearance as you go from day to day. You can make this easier by going back to thinking about the countless ways your body works to keep you strong, healthy, and alive. Even when you get sick or injured, your body automatically gets to work hard for you to pull through. So when you look at yourself in the mirror, always recognize how truly incredible your body is.

While you cannot change all these things overnight, now is a great time to make a start. Often, we feel insecure because we are our own toughest critic. But being only critical whenever we step in front of a mirror, makes those insecurities grow.

No matter where you are with self-love and acceptance at the moment, one step you can always take to make this journey easier is to make every mirror your friend.

If you are struggling with your self image and it's causing you to doubt yourself, or feeling unsure who you are at your core, refer back to this chapter often. Challenge your self-criticism. Improve your internal vocabulary. Make a list of the things you like about yourself, your skills, your strengths. Write down the things your body does that you find the most impressive. Stay patient and compassionate with your feelings and emotions. Say nice things. You can do this. You can love yourself.

So, don't hide from mirrors. Don't be afraid to face them. The person looking back at you will soon become a person you can truly appreciate.

STEP OUTSIDE YOUR SAFETY NET

YOUR PREDICTIONS AND FEARS CAN BE YOUR TOOLS

Another chapter down and a few more to go. You're doing great!

With each page you turn you are learning things that will help you become more empowered and courageous. In the previous chapters, you learned how to see your self-worth, start building a solid base for your confidence, and take a lot of time to reflect on who you are and who you want to be.

Next, let's take things a tad further by helping you step out of your safety net, also known as your comfort zone, and recognize when it's best to do it.

Your safety net is the behavioral space in which your activities and behaviors fit into a specific pattern or routine that ensures minimum risk and stress. This is why many people categorically refuse to ever leave that space—because they're so darn comfortable! While in your comfort zone, you generally know what to do, what to expect, and it's easier to predict the consequences of your actions. Naturally, if you are in this zone each day, you won't feel any kind of stress unless something unexpected happens.

But you want to change, right? You want to be able to stand your ground, stand by your ideas and feel more comfortable with yourself. And to do this, having the ability to leave the safety net behind is crucial. Because at one point or other, you will need to shake things up, take a risk, and prepare yourself to feel new things.

I know, sometimes even just the thought of escaping the safety net can be scary and daunting, especially if you have never done this before. However, this one step alone can empower you a lot, if you want your life to change.

Stepping out of the safety net will:

- Help you become more of a go-getter.

- Help you recognize and let go of things that aren't serving you or your progress (even when they're sentimental, cozy, or a bit of a crutch).
- Give you additional courage to take even more growth-promoting risks.
- Give you the strength to deal with the aftermath when sometimes things don't go as planned.
- Awaken your creativity.
- Help you embrace and like challenges, instead of running away from them.

But that's just a brief example. Chances are you'll discover so much more than that.

It's true that choosing to step out of your comfort zone will be difficult sometimes, but it's not impossible. As long as you don't push yourself too hard and keep in tune with your gut feelings and with reality, you will succeed.

What Are Your Predictions And Fears?

Before you start, let's do some more self-reflection. I know! I'm making it so obvious how strongly I feel about the importance of always knowing your starting point.

For this exercise, try to analyze what is keeping you from taking action. Think about the things that are holding you back and might be stopping you from even thinking about taking risks.

For many people (myself included), the most influential holdbacks are negative predictions and fears. These are the negative what-ifs, and the racing thoughts that have the ability to freeze you within your fears. It becomes so hard to take any action then. Like if you have a fear of confrontation, standing up to anybody will feel almost impossible. Or if your boss keeps giving you more work than it's humanly possible to bear, but you don't say anything for fear of getting fired. It's a suffocating feeling.

If you let too many of these things hold you back and influence you into inaction, most of the time things will become even harder in the long run. So the ability to decide and sometimes leave your safety net completely behind by taking on challenging action is one of the best ways you can grow. Even if you have some fears or insecurities to work through. Here are some steps to help you do this:

Know Your Why

It's important for you to get clear on the why behind each challenging action. Think about the result you want to achieve and paint a picture of it super strong, so that it has enough legs to carry you forward. If you can get your why to dwarf the fear and the possible friction the challenge might cause at first, then you're on the right track.

You can make a vision board to help you see things more clearly. Draw yourself inside a circle in the middle, and surround the picture of you with everything you want to achieve right now. From the bigger picture like gaining more confidence, overcoming insecurity or standing up for yourself, to the boiled-down specifics like proving to your boss your workload is far too much, and bringing a new proposed timetable you think would work so much better.

Creating a clear and positive why will help you clarify for yourself what exactly you want to gain from taking that risk, and from leaving your safety net just for a bit. Even though you might still be scared, you'll also realize the rewards waiting for you could be much greater. So keep your why specific, and impossible to resist.

Prepare To Feel Uncomfortable

All this will probably come with a bit of discomfort to say the least. But you don't have to be afraid of it. Remember that this feeling is normal for anyone planning to do the same thing. As long as you don't push yourself to the point of anxiety, some discomfort is to be expected, and it will eventually turn to excitement when you realize just how much you have done to question those insecurities and challenge those fears.

Talk To People Who Tried And Succeeded

If you're still on the fence, you can try reaching out to other people who have stepped out of their own comfort zones, and taken risks successfully.

Try to think of people in your life who have changed their lives for the better in some way. Go for a coffee and ask them how they found the courage and motivation to keep going. Even though their situations are different from yours, you might still be able to pick up a few tips that will help you with your own journey.

Don't Be Afraid To Fail

Failure shouldn't be the thing that stops you from moving forward. Try to see possible failure as a teacher you can learn from, to make your next steps easier. Failure is part of life. Even in situations when you do rely on your safety net heavily, there is still a possibility of failing. So don't be afraid of it.

Taking on the occasional challenge doesn't make failure any more or less likely. It just happens as it wants, really. So when it does, even though it might be hard at that moment, try to accept it as a life lesson, reflect on any possible reasons why, and see if there is anything you can take with you from the temporary setback, before you try again.

Have A Conversation With Yourself About Your Decision

Having said that, remember to make sure the action you're about to take is a reasonable one. Check in with yourself often to make sure you're keeping things real.

Depending on the size and life-dependency level of your decision, make sure to first have a backup, or a solid plan B to fall on. Set some other possible solutions in motion. Make sure your grandma has a free spare room, or that you have a nice side hustle running, or that you have a transferable-date return ticket. Measure everything twice.

Building Your Inner Courage

Throughout history, all the significant people who took groundbreaking action and made a mark on our lives and our futures, have had to choose to step out of their comfort zones and take incredible risks at one point or another.

In doing this, they transformed their own lives too, and made so much noise that the rest of the world noticed, and changed. But chances are, they were nervous, scared, anxious or doubtful too. Every step probably felt like 10 miles to them. They were only human as well.

So, however daunting and challenging a big decision might seem, whether it's a life decision or more of an everyday one, it's possible to face it and you can make it happen even if your knees shake as you walk. The important thing is that you walk.

You can't ever be brave without first feeling afraid.

Even if you have to cut a hole in that safety net just to get one foot out, do it. Only then will you be able to start working to break through the predictions and worries, and discover the reality of all the possibilities on the other side.

Always remember to take all the time you need. If it takes months or years, then so be it. Come prepared.

Here's how you can help build your courage:

Keep Your Mindset Sharp

Your mindset decides a lot. It is where your fears and uncertainties might be so ingrained that you feel frozen. Whenever you feel like you can't move an inch, go back to the positive twist exercise. If you're unsure about going out later, because you know someone who always challenges you will be there, and you're worried about the peer pressure, create a positive scenario in your mind as well. After all, the possibility of a positive outcome where you do stand up for yourself is 50/50, so cut yourself some slack.

Keep your possibilities at the forefront. Remember you can say no. Walk over to the friends you actually get on with, and talk to them instead. Keep your mindset focused on the outcome you want to achieve. Keep alert and present. Keep the voice in your head friendly. No compromises. Allow your mind to back you up.

Challenging your comfort zone to promote growth is a giant task that needs discipline and stamina. But once you show yourself that you can in fact do brave things, your mindset will on automation become more believing.

Take One Bold Step

If you find yourself in the cycle of hyping yourself up, and then losing your nerve when it's time to do something significant, you might want to change your tactics. Surprise yourself by taking just one bold step toward your goal to gain unexpected rewards.

If you're an entrepreneur and want to make some like minded friends, but normally get too nervous to go to meetups, this time get a ticket to the biggest event of the year. Then, don't give yourself the chance to question it. Block the day off in your calendar, get ready and go without thinking about it. Or, if you have always wanted to put your music on YouTube but are scared of people's comments, pick just two songs and upload them as a trial run, to see how you feel and how you really react when someone does comment.

Taking just one bold step you wouldn't normally do, that's already courage. And now you've woken it up, you'll feel it grow even more. It will spark up motivation to try more. The next steps won't be as difficult.

Learn How To Deal With Stress

Stress has enough power to put a stop to almost anything. What makes this harder is that stress is an inevitable part of life. Whatever we might try, there will be times when it's impossible to get rid of it completely. But, it's always possible to learn to manage it and keep it at bay.

Use different techniques like keeping a well organized calendar, trying meditation, stress-management apps, mind-clearing walks with the dog, movies, going raving. Find out what works for you. By reducing the stress you feel, taking risks won't feel as intimidating as it would if you were always stuck in stressful situations without addressing them.

Test Your Negative Predictions

Having negative predictions is another normal part of the decision making process. They can range anywhere from mild assumptions to the horror scenarios we've mentioned before.

If you're someone who tends to imagine and worry about possible negative outcomes a lot, it will help to note them down and sort them out just like you would do with anything else. So write everything down, even the smallest negative predictions that might come up when you're trying to make decisions or solve dilemmas.

Then, arrange your predictions by their difficulty level. If they were to come true, which one would be the easiest to deal with, and which one would be the most difficult? Next, test them one by one, starting with the easiest, and go as far as you will.

For example, if the first prediction on your list is failing to write a good piece about something you're experienced at, give writing it a try. If you like what you've written, that's your first negative prediction proved wrong. If your second prediction is your article being rejected by your favorite big blog, or a major publication, submit it anyway. Yep, they might reject it, but there's an equal chance they won't. And if they like it, then that's your second negative prediction proved wrong. Which means new inspiration to do more. So keep testing. You'll be surprised how far you can go.

Prioritize

Which action would feed into your overall goal or the desired bigger picture most directly right now?

Prioritization is such an underrated skill. If you have a set of tasks or a set of possible actions you'd like to take, always sort them out in your head according to how directly they feed into the reality you want to create for yourself.

That way, you'll always be clear on where you should start, and which action is currently the most likely to influence the outcome. Deal with them from the top. Keep the least influential for your downtime.

Keep Your Eyes On The Big Picture

Throughout this entire process, you'll probably need to say goodbye to some things you have been used to and comfortable with, habits that made you feel safe, and at times you might feel like you're struggling with that. That's fine, and everyone deals with that feeling whenever they're making some changes. It helps to always try to focus on your reason for wanting this change.

When you think about the future gains and how you're going to grow through the change, it will make you stronger and well equipped to keep going. With your big picture in your mind, go back to your vision board often and add to it, cherish the things you have put on it that you've already accomplished.

This will help you let go of the old habits which don't contribute to this big picture anymore, and you'll feel more confident about each decision you make and each problem you resolve.

Level Up Now!

Level up your reality through building your courage and stepping out of your safe space as best you can. Because by doing so, you will be learning about yourself, surprising yourself, discovering new layers of you that maybe you didn't know were even there.

Just keep going and before you know it, you will be living a life different to the one you are used to now.

What Are Your Safety Behaviors?

At this point, you already understand what your safety zone is and why it needs to be abandoned sometimes. All of this is a lot to take, so just try to remember that you want to keep going at your own comfortable pace. Burnout won't get you there any faster, so be mindful of your energy levels, your momentary limits, and some things you might be more sensitive about than others. This is an experience deeply personal to you.

Now, let's go through some examples of real-life safety behaviors and how they may manifest on the outside:

- Finding it hard to go anywhere without your friends. You might not even get coffee or pick up a pizza when no one is around.
- Completely avoiding situations and places that you know could compromise your comfort, challenge you, or make you feel exposed.

- Wearing layers of clothes so that you don't feel exposed.
- Wearing layers of clothes when you are insecure about your body, even when it's hot outside.
- Always wearing sunglasses to avoid eye contact or cover your emotions.
- Creating a mental escape route plan as soon as you get to a bar or an event. Always keeping aware of the fire exits.
- Always sitting at the back at classes to avoid being called by the professor or asked for your opinion or knowledge.
- Making up excuses or entire stories when you feel uncomfortable and want to leave, instead of just saying you feel uncomfortable and want to leave.
- Struggling to share stories from your personal life with most people, and always turning the conversation back to focus on the other person instead.
- Avoiding speaking up in meetings at work, even when you know a lot about the topic.
- Struggling to share your ideas or changes to workflow processes that you know could work a lot better.
- Always avoiding confrontation or attention, even in cases where it could be beneficial or needed, and rather getting on with things the way you always have.

Add anything else you might have noticed while thinking about this:

- ....
- ....

If you recognize and acknowledge that you might be relying on some of these behaviors, or similar, to keep yourself on the safe side and avoid confrontation, it's a great first step towards working on changing them, or letting them go. By becoming more comfortable and confident with yourself, you won't need to turn to safety behaviors to feel better quite so often anymore.

Because they come with a catch.

Even though safety behaviors might seem like they work well in the moment, it's been proven that long term, they can actually be harmful to your confidence, slow down your personal and professional progress, and some of them could even cause more anxiety instead of getting rid of it.

So, if you're recognizing some safety behaviors in your own habits, it's best to start taking small steps to gradually reduce them. This doesn't have to be daunting. For example, if you're always quiet in zoom meetings because you're worried you'll say something awkward, you can start by picking up the meeting agenda the night before. Pick just one topic that's scheduled to be talked about (always one you know a lot about—if there isn't a topic you feel you're strong at, wait for next week). Then, promise yourself you'll contribute to the conversation about this topic at least once tomorrow. Write down a list of points you think will be discussed or will be relevant to the topic, keep it on your desk, and then use them the next day when your topic comes up.

Just one contribution is an awesome start! And once you've done this a few times, it will become so much easier to start contributing to other topics as and when they come up.

Make a similar action plan for each of your safety behaviors. Be easy on yourself, but do try as hard as you can to stick to the things you set up to do. The more acclimatized you get, the more you add. This way you'll learn to challenge the safety behaviors that might feel nice but are holding you back. And you'll challenge them in a healthy way that's also realistic, and won't be so daunting that it sees you run back to your safety nest straight away.

Beat Fear Of Failure

Fear of failure is a super common fear a lot of people experience when facing big changes and smaller everyday decisions alike. So once you feel like you're standing a bit stronger in your shoes, it's time to start digging a bit deeper into this tricky fear. As with the previous step, remember to monitor yourself closely and move forward at your own pace. But it is important to explore this fear a bit further and think about the possible triggers behind it. Understanding it just that little bit more will help you find some ways to overcome it.

Fear of failure is an indirect fear, which means it's connected to your expectations and anticipations, rather than a solid, primal threat. It likes to feed on suspicions, possibilities and imagination. Yet it still feels super real to us. But the good thing about indirect fears is they can be challenged.

One fun way of challenging fear of failure is using your curiosity.

We're all born curious, and for a good reason. Curiosity moves us forward. It's the reason you solve some problems better than others. It's behind your hobbies and passions. It makes you seek answers and brainstorm ideas. In fact, curiosity is why we all know what gravity is. It's why light bulbs turn on at a flick of a switch, or why Google exists. Amazing, when you think about it!

And all you need to do is give it more space. Whenever you notice you're avoiding something for the fear of a possible negative outcome, use this formula:

> *Fear of failure = possible negative outcome < Curiosity = possible amazing outcome*

Keeping things honest, you can analyze the possible negative outcome you're worried about, and compare it with the drive you have to also find out how positive the outcome could be.

Give it a chance. Remember, it's usually 50/50 (unless you're absolutely sure you don't have the brain for maths, and so definitely can't resolve that logarithm). But when your opportunities are open and there is an equal chance of failure and success, your curiosity can take a strong lead and reveal many opportunities for growth, ideas, life lessons, and happiness.

Don't stop yourself from trying because you're afraid the outcome might be a disaster. Even the most legendary people in the world have made mistakes. And when mistakes do happen, try seeing them as feedback. It wasn't meant to be this time, but next time, it won't stop you from experiencing something amazing. Keep choosing what is more important than fear until it becomes a habit.

Overcome Self-Doubt

Apart from fear, any self-doubt you might be experiencing could also be a big factor keeping you in your comfort zone. Self-doubts simply won't allow enough courage to come through for you to take action. Self-doubts also tend to thrive when your inner voice is overly critical, and when the way you see yourself is somewhat fragile. Therefore, a lot of what we've covered in previous chapters will come useful here, like the criticism-challenging exercises, changing your internal dictionary and making your inner voice nicer and much more friendly, or fostering a more compassionate and positive self image.

Refer back to those sections as often as you need. In effect, they'll also help you let go of the doubts you might have about yourself or your skills, and to move forward.

Here are a few more tips to help you do this:

- Whenever something challenging happens, be aware of your inner critic so that you can stop any unkind thoughts before they come out.
- Ask yourself, if this is a rational doubt, actually based on something solid, or is it an indirect fear based on expectation? If the doubt is honestly rational, what can you do to challenge or improve it?
- Keep reminding yourself of the great things you've done or achieved, any big or small victories, and successes. Remind yourself of your strengths and things you're really good at. How can you use them to grow from this situation?
- Try not to focus on what other people are thinking of you. As long as you're accountable to yourself, and open to objective and constructive feedback from people who actually care about you, you're good.
- Make a point of spending more time with people who uplift you, support you, and like you as you are. Spend less time where you're tolerated, and more time where you're celebrated. I love this saying, because it's so true! Everyone deserves to be celebrated for who they are, their journey, their imperfections, their talents. You deserve it too.
- Be supportive of yourself too, even when some of your decisions turn out not to be what you expected. Even when you're having a bad day and cannot face any challenges, any mind exercises, not even this book. It's totally ok. You're human. Bad days don't

last forever and you will feel stronger again soon. Be nice to yourself and have your back whatever happens.

Challenge Perfectionism

Trying to be perfect all the time can be another type of safety net. It's also incredibly hard. And yet, many of us are too familiar with the kind of perfectionism that effectively ties our hands.

It's the kind of perfectionism that makes you wait forever, instead of taking action. You wait for the perfect time, situation, place, or a million other things before doing something significant. Or you might be extremely anxious before submitting an application form, a thesis, a piece of writing or a video somewhere important, because you keep nitpicking and finding all these imperfections. You feel like the piece is never finished. So you might not send or upload it at all. And then you'll never know what could have been.

In reality, perfection rarely comes. And it's overrated, really.

Because no matter the situation, we learn a whole lot more about each other's uniqueness and character through imperfections.

Even if it's a super serious job interview. It's the hiccups that let us know about someone's true essence. It's how you deal with or react to those hiccups that lets other people know you're quick and sharp with your ideas, or funny, or highly creative, or a quick learner, or able to take ownership. Life's imperfections can often make a lot of things work in our favor.

Big artists also often think their work is imperfect. Da Vinci spent years painting the Mona Lisa, and allegedly he was never happy with it. Sources say Andy Warhol would seek reassurance from his friends about his work every single day, before he could continue with it. If they waited for their art to be perfect, it would likely never even see the light of day.

So, more often than not, striving for utter perfection doesn't always promote the best outcome. Here's a few tips to challenge the darker side of perfectionism when you need to:

- Acknowledge if your perfectionism is on the side of unhealthy by keeping you from taking important action for far too long.
- Believe in yourself, and believe you can make big dreams happen (because you can!), but always keep your nearest goals and milestones close to reality and reflective of your current situation. That way, it will be much easier to stay on track and keep moving, as your milestones stay within reach. Whenever your next goal seems to be so far around the corner you can't even see it anymore, add another one in between, one that's smaller, but feeds into the bigger goal.
- Keep in mind feelings of uncertainty are normal, and everyone has them when they're on the verge of change. Pay attention to them, but always remember these feelings don't necessarily mean something's

wrong with your work or with your decisions. Sure, read through your paper five times, give it the most you possibly can, but then it's time. Time to hit the submit button.
- Share your thoughts, work or dilemmas with other people, especially when it comes to big changes. While you know you can trust your decisions, it's often beneficial to get someone else's perspective as well. Choose people who are rational and give you good constructive criticism and encouragement. Choose people who'll share their thoughts, but also inspire you to make things happen the way *you* want.
- Ask yourself what's the worst that could happen, and reflect on this question honestly. It'll make it easier to assess your decision and clearly line up the things you are willing to risk or accept, and those you aren't.

CREATE YOUR NEW MINDSET POWERZONE

YOUR STRENGTH, YOUR DECISIONS, YOUR POWER

Ah, the mind.

How powerful it is, and how much pressure it can actually take!

Did you know the human brain changes its physical shape as a result of learning?

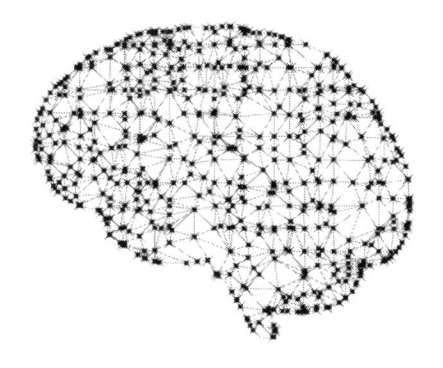

It's true!

It's called structural neuroplasticity. When your brain undergoes changes or absorbs new information, it creates brand new neural pathways to accommodate for the change. It can even move functions from one area to the other, whenever things become too crowded.

Guess what this means: If you've learned anything from this book, your brain must have slightly changed its shape since you first opened it.

Fascinating. And, great work!

This is yet another incredible piece of evidence showing how truly powerful your mind is. When you think about how your brain can actually transform and restructure itself, it becomes much easier to believe that your mind is also powerful enough to overturn the thinking and habitual patterns that might have been holding back your self-esteem, your resilience, your progress.

It *can* change your life.

Working with your mind and changing how you see and think about yourself will influence your actions, and therefore your reality and your world. In fact, you've come so far in this book you've likely started to observe some of those effects already. And if not, that's ok too. Just keep paying close attention as you work through the exercises and remember, your individual experience is unique.

There's still more to learn. Keep this in mind as you continue reading.

Your Mindset Powerzone

Your mindset refers to your own core assumptions and view of the world. It is the lens you use to see the outside world and evaluate it. Right now, your mindset might still be more or less on the fence, or just leaning towards the direction you want it to lean, to start gaining more healthy confidence. That's ok because there are so many more things you can do to foster this positive mindset change to make you a more confident person.

Generally, there are two types of mindsets people have:

Fixed mindset

People with this mindset believe their attributes and fortunes cannot be changed. No matter what they do, they believe there is no long term and effective way for them to improve their skills, emotional intelligence, personality, luck, and so on. Therefore, people with a fixed mindset will feel reluctant to do anything to improve and develop their life. They're not usually open to facing new challenges because they don't think there's a point. Also, with a fixed mindset, people may believe they can only succeed if there is a proven path walked a thousand times before. If they can't see it, why bother?

Growth mindset

The growth mindset is where people believe they can improve their fortune, knowledge, emotional intelligence, skills and other attributes with experience and time. They believe they can change so they will always seek ways to make their life better and work hard for the things they want to achieve. They don't mind putting in the extra effort because they know it will pay off. And even if it doesn't, they accept they'll at least learn something from it. Fostering the growth mindset creates a positive cycle of thought patterns and behaviors, which eventually lead people to achievements and the acquisition of new skills.

So… Which one would you rather have?

I think I can guess the answer.

But!

If you feel like you might be stuck within the fixed mindset, or leaning towards it at the moment, don't worry about it. There are things you can do to work on unfixing it. Here's how you can start transforming your mindset into one that allows for growth:

- Think about the value of your journey and the possibilities within it, which will enable you to realize your why and your real reasons for wanting to change, and to keep them strong enough to carry you through the actual action-taking process.
- Pay close attention to your thoughts and words, especially whenever they're geared towards yourself and your abilities. When you notice they tend to lean on negativity and doubt, make a conscious effort to change that, using some of the earlier exercises in this book. Try to find a positive twist for every

negative prediction and allow yourself to indulge in the thought of that good possibility for a while.
- Instead of settling on negative thoughts (even when at the moment they might actually be realistic), end them with the word 'yet'. If you're struggling with a task and your mind is saying you should just give up because you simply can't do it, change this thought to "I can't do this, just yet." This leaves things open ended, and acknowledges the option to learn what you need to learn to complete the task at a later stage.
- Stay motivated to test your abilities and commit to giving yourself the chance to surprise yourself. Challenge the fixed mindset by testing its borders and see how far out you can venture beyond them. Once you start doing this, you'll also start enjoying pushing things even further, and every test you set for yourself that later proves your true capabilities will become fuel. A blast for your confidence. And motivation to keep going.

Staying Grounded

Staying grounded is equally important.

Fostering a growth mindset is great but if you cannot stay grounded amidst the chaos the change might create, you will easily get overwhelmed. Keeping your mindset grounded means you remain in control of your mind. Rather than allowing external factors to control you, a grounded mindset lets you keep on top of your thoughts, emotions, and everything else during any change or a challenging time.

It proves useful when you're waiting for crucial exam results, or when you're waiting to hear back about the dream job application you sent last week, or biting your nails as you send your first submission to a digital design competition.

If you often find yourself easily swayed by other people's emotions (like when everyone in the office panics at the next big deadline being suddenly changed to 'by the end of today'), if you're a natural empath, or get affected quite easily by negative news, learning how to keep a grounded mindset comes in handy too.

It keeps you (a bit more) sane.

Create Room To Grow Supportive Roots

Cherish the person you are but with your mind always open to change. This goes hand in hand with accepting any current reality for what it is. It doesn't mean you're surrendering or giving up at all. Rather, it's a big part of keeping in check with your rational consciousness, and staying grounded.

From the beginning, we have focused on learning how to love and accept yourself for who you are. Even if you want to change some things about yourself, you should still cherish yourself from the start, and all the way throughout the process. Watching out for yourself and being compassionate towards your whole being regardless of the things you perceive as perfect or imperfect, will create a rock-solid base to stand on when the rest of the ground gets rocky.

And your unconditional support will make a huge difference for your future self, too. Keep an open mind for the person you are aiming to become in the future. Never underestimate your own strength and avoid looking to others for approval which in most cases, you don't actually need.

This will create space for your confidence to grow some more roots. Once that happens, it will be easier to stay put through a challenge that would have previously caught you off-guard. You'll feel less doubt, less temptation to hide. You'll be able to come up with a constructive plan. You'll trust yourself more.

Disconnect When You Need To

Recognizing when it's a good time to disconnect is always important, but it's especially crucial when building healthier self-esteem, for a few reasons:

It's easy to get so used to being around other people, online or offline, that we sometimes forget how to be on our own. A surprising amount of people find it super hard to spend time with only themselves. They're so used to constant distractions and assurances from friends or followers, always absorbing external influences, voices, opinions. They don't even know how to think for themselves anymore. They lose track of what's important and valuable to them as individuals.

That's why learning how and when to take time away and be alone is a total essential.

It could be a daily walk without taking your phone out of your pocket. Or time you spend reading what you want, listening to your kind of music. It could be taking a daily half-an-hour to just sit in your apartment, stare out the window and let your thoughts process themselves. Or it could be a week in an AirBnb. A month backpacking. Whatever spending enjoyable time alone might look like for you.

Being comfortable and at ease in your own company is a skill, and a really positive one. It's an advantage. It's extremely beneficial not only for your confidence, but for your overall wellbeing as a unique human being too. It keeps you in tune with your own moral compass, your own values, preferences, likes, ideas, feelings, and opinions.

On top of that, learn to recognize when you're getting overwhelmed by social media or by spending too much time online in general. This of course depends heavily on your work projects, creative projects, things you study or are invested in, but always stay aware of how you're feeling and allow yourself to take five if you notice signs of burnout.

As for social media, as creative and inspiring as they can be, they can also create pressure, toxicity, negative feelings of inadequacy, or a rather urgent dependency on external validation (likes, compliments, views, shares). Being overwhelmed by all this is just a start, and it can possibly develop into something more serious. So when you start noticing any of the above in yourself, or if you often leave social media feeling off, or defeated, or bad about yourself, it's ok to take a break for a while.

It might feel weird at first, as you'll have an almost involuntary urge to tap the icons when scrolling through your phone, and you might get fomo, but if you resist and stick to the break, you'll start feeling better quickly. The break can be a couple of days, a week, a few months. Anything works.

Before I'd jumped back on social media because of my books, I was on a continuous detox for a couple of years. I completely deleted one profile, and kept a couple of others, but wasn't active on any of them. And I can honestly say I didn't even miss them after a while. It gave me so much new space to focus on my life, my projects, my relationship, my family, my friends, my creativity, the cats, everything. I'd felt more grounded in my life and in my decisions (and their consequences), than I did for years before that.

A big part of what made the disconnecting easier was knowing the decision didn't have to be permanent. So always keep that in mind. If you set a week's worth of detox, you know it's temporary and it will help you stick to it. And even if you decide to try detoxing from social media indefinitely, always remember it doesn't have to be forever. Keep your options open and your mind sensitive to how you're truly feeling day by day. Explore what can happen. Keep it real.

If you're an entrepreneur or a creator and social media is part of your work and process, it helps to focus on creating more than you consume. Only consume when you need to network, and limit even that to just the accounts and collabs that are actually worth your attention and energy.

Fine-Tune Your Decision-Making Process

If you often feel overpowered by decision making, it doesn't matter if you're choosing between two meals on a menu, two pairs of jeans, or where to live for the next few years of your life. It can all be equally daunting sometimes.

But for life's bigger decisions, you can make the process easier and more realistic with an analysis or a checklist. A mind map can help too. It might sound basic, but even a small honest analysis will take some pressure off the dilemma, and will make your decision more grounded in effect. You can build your own personal decision checklist or a mind map around these bullet points:

- The main goal and purpose of the decision.
- The pros and cons you think each option will bring. Create a color-code for the cons—red for the possibilities you're the least willing to accept, green for the ones you can see yourself facing.
- An outline of the steps you'll need to take before and after each option. Leave room to account for unforeseen steps or consequences as well. You can color-code these steps the same way, to give yourself an idea which outline seems realistically more manageable for you and any other people who might be directly affected by, or dependent on your decision.

- A realistic backup plan for each of your options. Complete this with the steps you'll need to take to set this backup plan firmly in place before you go ahead with the main decision.

Keep your analysis as honest as you can, and it will offer you space to stay grounded while listening to your gut feelings and considering your wants and dislikes. You'll nurture a mindset that allows for growth while keeping your head out of the clouds. Don't get me wrong, you should definitely sneak a good peek into the clouds, into your ideal, what you wish for and dream of, into the world you want to create for yourself. Just remember to always come back to where you are, to your starting point. Because only from there you can actually start moving.

Art Of Positive Psychology

Positive psychology focuses on behaviors and character strengths that accommodate building habits, patterns and thinking processes to help people create a positive purpose and meaning in their everyday lives.

We can also use some of the cognitive and habitual positive psychology techniques to nurture a friendly space for us to grow more confidently. Through positive psychology, you will no longer just seek survival methods, but you will do everything you can to thrive and flourish.

The key pillars of positive psychology are:

Positive Emotional States

This can include nurturing warmth, pleasure, feel-good memories, comfort, love, forgiveness, or gratitude. It means allowing yourself to indulge, savor positive moments, self-care, and enjoyment, when you can.

Flow

The state of flow and full engagement happens when you're doing activities you're genuinely interested in and activities that you get wholeheartedly absorbed in. This can include creative projects, the type of work that's truly meaningful to you and provides gratification beyond money, and also the things you just love to do for fun.

Meaning And Purpose

This is a satisfaction of a personal nature, which is fulfilled when something you do or achieve deeply serves and aligns with your personal moral compass and values. It's the feeling you get when you contribute selflessly to a cause or a project that's so close to your heart you don't care about any other benefits you might get from completing it. It's the feeling you have when you know you're part of something greater than yourself.

Accomplishment

The act of having fulfilled or accomplished something you strived for. Either professionally, creatively or personally, this will usually have a tangible reward attached to it, like an award, the new home you've always wanted, a grant for that innovative idea you've been developing, or seeing pretty much anything you've been striving for or working on, become a reality.

Positive Relationships

This means creating and nurturing a network of *your* people. Where you can help it, you surround yourself with people who uplift you, share the same passions and interests, give you a creative buzz, or just generate a lot of love and positivity in you simply for who they are. Being with them is easy. You can be 100% yourself. They can see all versions of you without you feeling exposed. They can see all versions of you, and appreciate and accept that's who you are.

At first, these pillars might seem slightly too good to be true, maybe even unattainable. But they are all completely realistic and possible. In fact, nurturing just some parts of them, the parts that are achievable for you now, will in itself raise your overall vibe. Others will notice it, and you will notice it too. You'll gain a new sense of your capabilities and a higher level of awareness. That alone might as well reveal a way to climb the rest of those pillars. To make a start, here are some steps to help you practice:

- Visualize yourself as a strong, confident, and positive person. Remember the power of your mind and use this to convince yourself that you are all these things. Because you are.
- Keep up that confident vibe you learned about in

Chapter 3. Even on the days you aren't feeling particularly strong or confident, keeping up with the appearance of it will always serve you better than sulking (definitely do that when you need to, but not for too long). You'll feel different tomorrow, and might benefit from the opportunity you created today by keeping some swagger in your step when you needed to. Sometimes, putting up a bit of a show is worth it.

- Allow yourself to be human, make mistakes, take risks, and learn through experiences. Appreciate and celebrate having overcome any challenge.
- Always remember there's nothing wrong with asking for help. When you're surrounded by more of your people, don't be afraid to be more honest and open with them, and ask them to help you out whenever you need actual help or just moral support.
- Notice what puts you in the flow state of mind, and make some room for it in your daily or weekly schedule.
- The goal isn't to ignore unpleasant or negative emotions, but rather to gain a better understanding of what makes you feel more yourself and flourish as a person, and put a lot more intention and emphasis on that.
- Create some more positive interventions and make space for at least one each day. Apart from the obvious ones like the gratitude notes, you could create a few that are more specific to you, and will

give your mindset a positive boost. Find out what makes you tick and make it your daily tonic.

The commitment you'll need to make is not a commitment to certain change, goal, challenge, or detox. It's making a commitment to yourself. Your growth. And deciding to embrace all the things that are good for you, and true to you.

When you do that, you're making a commitment to your individuality, your uniqueness, your values. It's the most important commitment you'll ever make in your life.

That's the real mindset powerzone.

GET THE MOST OUT OF CHANGE

STANDING ON FIRM GROUND

Amazing stuff! You are almost there. Let's discover the last few bits of the puzzle.

As you learn and implement the strategies to help you transform into a more confident and self-reliant person, it will become all the more clear that the power to inspire, motivate and make change really does belong to you.

When you encounter situations where you'd previously feel like you have no choice but to stay silent and accept what other people want, now you'll see the sitch in a different light. Even if it involves discussing things with personalities usually stronger than yours. You will have learned the only true difference between you and them is the point of view. But not the ability to express it.

That's the kind of empowerment you will have prepared for yourself.

Of course, it's not always going to be easy, and your heart rate will probably still often increase to a thousand. Especially at the beginning. And sometimes, there will still be situations or encounters where it's definitely wiser to keep silent and walk the other way. But now you'll hesitate less, and have more trust in making those decisions.

If being unsure of yourself and feeling insecure has been your story for what feels like the longest time, and now you're starting to get strong glimpses of your new confidence, it's the most amazing feeling. So let's keep the momentum!

Because finding your ground is just the start. Your next job will be to stay on it, and create space to grow those strong confidence roots, remember?

So keep developing a positive, grounded growth mindset and a solid sense of self. Keep learning more about yourself, and how you can be more independent and self-reliant no matter where you are. Keep accepting who you are at each stage of your progress, respecting your decisions, and staying aware of your core values and preferences. Keep your mind open to compromise, but also think about when it's healthier not to. Keep exploring and building your courage.

It's a lot of work and it doesn't happen in an instant. So, hiccups are ok. Taking your time with it is definitely ok. Slower pace is always better than no pace at all.

The most important thing is to steady yourself in a good spot, keep balanced, and aim for some healthy and tangible progress.

Staying On Firm Ground

To make sure you've not only found your firm ground, but can actually stay there long term, you need to create a little bubble, a little insulation around you to make sure your new confidence space stays warm and welcoming. It will become the nurturing space from which you can repeatedly make the choice to keep learning and grow further from where you are now.

Because you've learned far too much to allow yourself to get discouraged. So, to keep some pace even through hiccups or occasions where your doubts might return and make a scene, you can always refer back to what you've already built. If you need to start again sometimes, then so be it.

Here are some exercises you can use to keep you on the right track and help make things go (mostly) smoothly:

Visualize Yourself As A Strong, Successful Person

Visualization can be awkward at first, but it works super well for a lot of people. You just imagine the version of yourself you want to become. What would that person do? How would they react? How would they express themselves? What is it they're most proud of? What's their next goal? What's their style and what they actually enjoy wearing?

Close your eyes and see that person. Watch them interact with the world and make choices for themselves. They are strong. They are confident. They are successful on their own terms.

Keep going back to that visualization of yourself, especially when you can't seem to find the motivation to go on. That person will be you. In fact, that person IS you. You just need to set them free. Sounds cheesy? Hell yeah! But it's also true.

Explore Affirmations

Have you tried using affirmations before?

People have somewhat split opinions about them. About half of the people who've tried using affirmations swear by them and can't imagine a morning or bedtime without them. The other half reported feeling rather indifferent, and said for an affirmation to be effective, it'd have to be super specific and speak directly to their heart.

So, same as some of the other practices and exercises we've been working through in this book, affirmations and their effectiveness will differ for each individual person. The only way to find out if they could work for you is to give them a try.

In a nutshell, affirmations are positive statements or reminders you listen to for motivation and encouragement. To start with, you can find plenty of positive affirmation sets online, free on YouTube or as audiobooks. They are usually designed for a variety of goals and situations you can choose from, like affirmations for anxiety, body positivity, self-esteem, courage, anti-stress, for studying, confidence at work, creativity, reflections before bed, and so much more. The options are endless.

You can choose a few sets of affirmations on different topics that apply to you, try listening to them every morning for a few days, and if you feel like they're working and make you feel more optimistic and uplifted, you can then go ahead and create your own personal sets. These will be even more effective as they'll apply specifically to your own challenges. Or invest in advanced audiobook affirmation sets, with combined topics and enough affirmations to last you a lifetime.

Foster A Love Of Learning

Finding some things you are passionate about and love learning about, and adding them to your set of milestones will do a great job in keeping you moving. Having multiple areas of interest gives you plenty of space to keep growing and progressing even if you find yourself stuck in one or two of them.

It's a bit like the writer's block. When I get it, it helps me so much to have multiple projects going on at the same time. Because it takes completely different states of mind to write a book like this one, or a horror story, or an article about minimalism. And there will be days when I absolutely cannot do one or the other. So it helps me to keep multiple writing projects open, because there's always one my mind *can* work on. That way I can make sure I always keep moving. And I find that my mindset always changes, and there always comes a time where I am able to return to the project I couldn't even face looking at last week.

And your mind works similarly when approaching your own projects. So make sure your vision board is full of variety, and your learning or working options are open.

Set reachable and realistic goals in each of those different areas, so that you are able to choose according to how you're feeling each day, where possible—don't miss important deadlines! Sometimes we have no choice. But when you do, this kind of prioritizing will set you up for more success, because you're not forcing yourself to do something you're not in the mood for. Just keep the options and ideas coming.

Brush Off Rejections

Just like mistakes, rejections are a part of life. You will be rejected by people, you will be rejected for jobs you apply for, your creativity and ideas will sometimes be rejected too. It's hard, and it definitely sucks, but try not to take these rejections too personally. Because more often than not, they have absolutely nothing to do with you. Rather, they are a reflection of the other party, their preferences, and their vision.

It doesn't matter who you are. You could be an extremely talented actor, writer, painter, designer, sound engineer, chef, singer, film producer, and still face rejection often. Steven Spielberg was rejected from The University of Southern California, School of Theater, Film and Television three times. And you've probably heard about J.K. Rowling, who was (now famously) rejected by not just one, but *twelve* publishers before her work became a worldwide phenomenon.

Sometimes you'll get feedback, other times you'll have absolutely no idea why they rejected you. But always remember, that was just one try. Focus on your next try, your next option. Find another door. Even if it takes twenty tries, never give up on a project, or on your talent, or on your vision.

Same goes for your self-esteem and confidence goals. Here, it's especially important to stick to compassion. Because it's somehow even easier to feel hurt when the effort you made to find the courage and speak up about an issue or be assertive at work, results in rejection by your friends or boss. But even if your ideas or opinions aren't met with understanding sometimes, it doesn't mean they don't matter. And it definitely doesn't mean you voicing them wasn't successful. People will still have noticed your effort. And it's still your personal win, because you've challenged yourself to do something you wouldn't do two weeks or two months ago. So give yourself the credit and appreciation you deserve.

After all, you've just challenged yourself, left your safety net behind and stepped up. Well done!

Stand Up For Others

Remember how Jackie Chan said he only ever found the courage to stand up to his bullies when he saw the new kid in his class being targeted in the same way?

For most people, helping others can be just as powerful as working on their own confidence and progress. In fact, it has been scientifically proven that helping others helps us. In one study, volunteering just once a week in a local soup kitchen helped the participants retain more resilience, and manage their stress better.

When you have found some confidence, you can use it to help others too. You can try joining a local community project, and see where it takes you. Or you could get involved when you see someone at work or a friend being treated unfairly. Look out for anyone you know who might be struggling with their confidence too.

What you do is totally up to you, and make sure you take your time with it until you feel comfortable and confident enough to do it effectively. By reaching out to others you will empower yourself as well as the people around you. And it feels amazing, too. Like the feeling you get when you make your best friend laugh, or drag them out of a rotten mood, times ten.

Feeling Proud Of Yourself Is Great!

There's nothing wrong with being proud of yourself.

You absolutely can take pride in your growth and what you accomplish. It will do even more wonders for your self-confidence and self-worth. So, be proud of every step you take no matter how small it might seem. By doing this, you will propel yourself much further than you might think.

Because being proud of yourself doesn't have to mean you're a show-off. When you keep things at a healthy, humble level, it will be so empowering. It will make you feel more grateful, it will make you feel more passionate, and it will keep you feeling motivated too. So if you accomplish something, don't be shy and acknowledge that you've done something great. Share it with your best friend, write about it in your journal, pin it on your vision board as a reminder. Owning your successes and victories is just as important as owning up to anything else. If this is something you're not used to doing, here are some tips to help you out:

As Usual, Make A List :)

I know, the endless lists! But they really work. Because as always, seeing your own thoughts materialize in front of you in black and white just helps put everything into a much clearer perspective.

And when you write down all the things you've done so far that you're feeling great about right now, it will enable you to fully acknowledge them, and to get used to creating positive praise in your mind for your successes.

Jot down all the things you have done in the past, or since you've started reading this book, or just today, that you think you should or could be proud of. This is another self-reflective way to help you learn about yourself even more. Allow yourself to feel amazing about everything you've done that's lit in your own eyes. Allow yourself to feel amazing about who you are, and who you are becoming.

Keep Your Self-Worth Strong

When you're done with your list, go through each point one by one. Remember the times when you have accomplished those goals or taken those steps, and how you felt. This will help you strengthen the way you see yourself even more. Even when you might have had self-doubts before, or still get them now sometimes (which is ok, as everything takes time). But now that you clearly see how many things you can be proud of, you will also feel stronger and assured about yourself and your skills. After all, you are amazing, so it's about time you noticed it more often!

Remember what we said earlier about love and appreciation? How they are the most powerful when they come from you first? Self-love is a big part of looking after your wellbeing and your mind. You are unique and different and just as there are many things you can be proud of, there are also many things you can find to love about yourself.

Keep Doing What You CAN

While it's always great to try your best in everything that you do, you should also keep in mind to be easy on yourself, take your time if you need it, and ask for help if you need it.

Focus on doing what you can. Even if you know that you aren't the best at something, you don't have to shy away from it completely. Like if you're great at coding, but visual design is not your strength, it doesn't mean you can't make a website. Do the stuff you can do, and for the rest of it, find a way to work with someone else.

If you think about it, none of the biggest projects that were a result of life-changing ideas, ever came to actual existence by just one person. Even if the one person starting them was a genius. In the vast majority of cases it does take a team of people to make big ideas see the light of day. Even the most solitary artists, inventors, or entrepreneurs are always inspired by *someone*. And even when they aren't at first, somewhere down the line they will eventually need someone to get involved to give the project the wings it needs.

So never think you can't achieve or complete something just because you don't own all the pieces of the puzzle. Just get started with what you know, and as your work evolves you will find a way. You will find people (other geniuses) who have the skills you need but don't have yet, and the odds are high your collab will give the project another dimension you might wouldn't have thought of otherwise.

Always make sure you keep enough space for your passions. If you choose to do things that you are naturally passionate about, you're bound to excel in them. Taking pride in what you do and following your passions go hand-in-hand. Your passion projects also feed your sense of self expression, fulfillment, and creativity, so keep up with them even if there aren't any material benefits at the moment. The point is to keep your soul fed, and to add some lightness to your heart. Both these things are equally as important as all the other successes you're pursuing. And when you can do both, you'll notice feeling more satisfied overall.

Be The Person You Need

All that said, always carry around with you a healthy dose of self-reliance.

Learning to be more self-reliant is a continuous quest, and it's one of the most powerful life skills you can possibly acquire.

Yes, do ask for help when you need it, work with others, love your circle of friends. But always make sure you're offering yourself the most you possibly can, too. Be your own rock. Be your own back-up. Trust your gut feeling and your judgment. Keep building your strength, your knowledge, your real life survival skills, and your dream life too.

And always remember it's ok to be human.

Especially in the most difficult situations, offer yourself as much support and compassion and love you would offer your best friend.

You so deserve your place on this planet. You deserve love. You deserve everything you want.

So work on it, and once you have it, rock it!

KUDOS: LOOK HOW FAR YOU'VE REACHED

Wow!

That was a lot to go through and yet, you are still here. You've reached the end of the book, and with it, hopefully a new sense of confidence. Awesome job!

Finding the confidence to stand your ground and be supportive of yourself is not an easy thing. But you've stuck by your decision and powered through each chapter, and now you have this whole new awareness. In fact, you probably are a slightly different person than the person you were when you first opened this book and read the introduction. Including the actual shape of your brain. No kidding!

Which is the goal we've set at the very start. Of course, you can't really learn anything overnight. You must first gain a more profound understanding of yourself and your starting point, so that you know exactly what you need to change to achieve your goal. This is what we discussed in the first two chapters. Chapter 1 was all about discovering who you were at the moment and why you need or want to work on yourself. Then in Chapter 2, we continued the discovery by focusing on and learning more about confidence and self esteem.

Next, we tackled a very real and difficult issue many people around the world have to deal with. Whether bullying happens online or in the real world, there are exercises and strategies you can use to help you stand up for yourself. If you, or someone you know has been affected by clockwork bullying, Chapter 3 offered some ways to help you overcome this problem and come out victorious.

In Chapter 4, you learned how to break any negative cycles you or your mind may be trapped in. Here, you learned essential things like setting your boundaries, prioritizing self-care, incorporating positive twists, transforming how you talk to yourself, and more to help you feel more comfortable and stronger in who you are.

Then in Chapter 5 we moved on to body positivity, and how important it is to start appreciating your body as it has done and continues to do so much for you. It's always there for you no matter what happens. Learning to love your body is a huge part of healthy self esteem and confidence growth. Regardless of what you perceive as perfection (and it's totally ok to want to change something), your body still deserves respect and appreciation at any stage of your life or journey.

In Chapter 6, we discussed the importance of learning to leave your safety net behind sometimes, and stepping out of your comfort zone. You need to do this as the person you want to become might not be residing in that comfort zone at all. To grow more confidence in yourself and your decisions, it's good to shake things up, start believing in yourself more and make sure you have the ability and backup to deal with what comes after.

Chapter 7 focused on your mindset. Your mind is incredibly powerful. If you can set your mind to target the changes you want to make, you will be able to make those changes. This is where self-motivation and positive psychology will help you out too.

And in Chapter 8 we brought everything together as we talked about how you can stay on the firm ground and be proud of yourself for it. So now, the ball is in your court. Reference back to this book as often as you need. Continue applying everything you have learned and challenging yourself even further and soon, you'll realize you are the new, future you. Good luck!

Feel free to drop me an email at mia@mia-reyes.com. I check it often. You can also join other readers of my books in our Facebook group:

https://www.facebook.com/groups/groundbreakercrew

And you can also share your thoughts about this book and how it helped you with other readers by leaving a quick review on Amazon.

Scan here for instant access to the *Stand Your Ground* review page:

REFERENCES

10 Tips to Overcome Self-Doubt. (2020, October 29). Eugene Therapy. https://eugenetherapy.com/article/overcome-self-doubt/

10 Ways to Step Out of Your Comfort Zone. (2015, April 15). Virtues for Life. https://www.virtuesforlife.com/10-ways-to-step-out-of-your-comfort-zone/

Abadi, M. (2017, December 12). *9 Wildly Successful People Who Were Bullied as Kids.* Business Insider. https://www.businessinsider.com/successful-people-who-were-bullied-2017-12?r=US&IR=T

Ackerman, C. E. (2018, June 25). *Self-Motivation Explained + 100 Ways to Motivate Yourself.* Positive Psychology. https://positivepsychology.com/self-motivation/

REFERENCES

Ackerman, C. E. (2019, July 3). *What is Self-Confidence? + 9 Ways to Increase It [2019 Update]*. Positive Psychology. https://positivepsychology.com/self-confidence/

Allan, P. (2019). *How to Handle Being Bullied as an Adult*. Lifehacker. https://lifehacker.com/how-to-handle-being-bullied-as-an-adult-1726099137

Anderson, R., Saulsman, L., McEvoy, P., Fursland, A., Nathan, P., & Ridley, S. (2012, November). *Overcoming Negative Predictions, Avoidance & Safety Behaviour*. Centre for Clinical Interventions. https://www.cci.health.wa.gov.au/-/media/CCI/Consumer-Modules/Building-Body-Acceptance/Building-Body-Acceptance--05--Overcoming-Negative-Predictions-Avoidance-Safety-Behaviours.pdf

Anonymous. (2014). *Answer to How Do I Avoid Being Bullied?* Quora. https://www.quora.com/How-do-I-avoid-being-bullied/answers/4872497?ch=10&share=7faf1070&srid=uGJtOC

BBC. (2018, April 24). *Stars Who Have Struggled With Their Confidence*. BBC; https://www.bbc.co.uk/programmes/articles/2zsGtF7RX3RRmLT9TbcH6sk/stars-who-have-struggled-with-their-confidence

Bernal, S. (2012, October 23). *How To Overcome Self-Doubt: 8 Tips to Boost Your Confidence*. Tiny Buddha. https://tinybuddha.com/blog/how-to-overcome-self-doubt-8-tips-to-boost-your-confidence/

Blumenthal, B. (2010, May 14). *5 Reasons to Stand up for Your Beliefs*. Sheer Balance. https://sheerbalance.com/5-reasons-to-stand-up-for-your-beliefs/

Bradford Brown, B. (1982). *The extent and effects of peer pressure among high school students: A retrospective analysis.* Journal Of Youth And Adolescence. https://link.springer.com/article/10.1007/BF01834708

Brenner, A. (2015). *5 Benefits of Stepping Outside Your Comfort Zone*. Psychology Today. https://www.psychologytoday.com/us/blog/in-flux/201512/5-benefits-stepping-outside-your-comfort-zone

Brotheridge, C. (2020, April 7). *7 Steps to Body Confidence*. Psychology Today. https://www.psychologytoday.com/us/blog/calmer-you/202004/7-steps-body-confidence

Brown, M. (2019, May 18). *9 Signs of Low Self-Esteem & 10 Ways to Grow Confidence*. The Couch: A Therapy & Mental Wellness Blog. https://blog.zencare.co/boost-self-esteem/

Bullying Myths and Facts. (n.d.). Bullying. https://www.bullying.co.uk/general-advice/bullying-myths-and-facts/

Busch, M. (2017, July 22). *8 Ways to Stop Being a Perfectionist*. May Busch. https://maybusch.com/8-ways-stop-being-perfectionist/

Carlson, N. (2013, December 23). *Elon Musk Was Bullied And Lonely As A Kid — Then He Found Computers And Business*. Business Insider. https://www.businessinsider.com/elon-musk-was-lonely-2013-12?r=US&IR=T

Cogborn, I. (2014, May 21). *Elizabeth Gilbert: The Connection Between Great Success and Great Failure.* Epiphany Institute. https://epiphanyinstitute.com/elizabeth-gilbert-ted-success-failure-connection/

Confidence. (2019). Psychology Today. https://www.psychologytoday.com/gb/basics/confidence

Cuncic, A. (2019). *3 Coping Strategies That Actually Make Anxiety Worse.* Verywell Mind. https://www.verywellmind.com/what-are-avoidance-behaviors-3024312

Cyber Bullying Advice. (2019). Bullying UK. https://www.bullying.co.uk/cyberbullying/what-is-cyberbullying/

Discovery Admin. (2017, October 19). *Common Misconceptions About Bullying.* Discovery Mood & Anxiety Program. https://discoverymood.com/blog/common-misconceptions-bullying/

Doleckova, M. (2020a, November 27). *How To Survive a Best Friend Heartbreak.* Medium. https://medium.com/fearless-she-wrote/what-to-do-if-you-struggle-with-female-friendship-dfe7c3af350b

Doleckova, M. (2020b, December 17). *Grow Your Mental Resilience to Stress Less About People's Opinions.* Medium. https://medium.com/publishous/grow-your-mental-resilience-to-stress-less-about-peoples-opinions-5e5c86457887

Doleckova, M. (2021a, February 24). *How Do You Know You're Ready to Make a Life-Changing Decision?* Medium. https://

medium.com/mind-cafe/how-do-you-know-youre-ready-to-change-your-life-87bd98ca5cab

Doleckova, M. (2021b, March 6). *To Live Your Best Life, Be More Curious Than You're Scared*. Medium. https://medium.com/curious/to-live-your-best-life-be-more-curious-than-youre-scared-10d4473b0c00

Doleckova, M. (2021c, March 21). *I Was Labeled "Too Skinny" When My Body Was Its Strongest*. Medium. https://medium.com/fearless-she-wrote/i-was-labeled-too-skinny-when-my-body-was-its-strongest-90acb9253a9c

Dornai, M. (2020, May 7). *Loving the Person in the Mirror*. Medium. https://mdornai.medium.com/loving-the-person-in-the-mirror-3ea3af1d7b51

Ellis, T. J. (2019, October 14). *7 Celebrities Who Started Out With Poor Self...* Theo J Ellis; https://theojellis.com/7-celebrities-who-started-out-with-poor-self-esteem/

Erickson, H. (2018, September 5). *Bullies Often Victims of Bullying Themselves, Research Shows*. SIU News. https://news.siu.edu/2018/09/090518-research-shows-bullies-often-victims-of-bullying.php

Fabrizio, L. (2016, August 8). *7 Steps to Stop Making Negative Assumptions*. Recovery Warriors. https://www.recoverywarriors.com/negative-assumptions/

Ferebee, A. (2019, September 23). *How to Stay Grounded in the Midst of Chaos (7 Dead Simple Strategies)*. Knowledge for Men.

https://www.knowledgeformen.com/how-to-stay-grounded/

Geoghegan, N. (2021, March 27). *How to Respond to an Adult Bully*. WikiHow. https://www.wikihow.com/Respond-to-an-Adult-Bully

George, C. (2014, June 6). *10 Ways To Step Out Of Your Comfort Zone And Overcome Your Fear*. Lifehack; https://www.lifehack.org/articles/communication/10-ways-step-out-your-comfort-zone-and-enjoy-taking-risks.html

Gifford, B. E. (2018, November 13). *Am I Being Bullied? 3 Types of Bullying Adults Face*. Counselling Directory. https://www.counselling-directory.org.uk/blog/2018/11/13/adult-bullying-how-to-tackle

Gordon, S. (2013, January 30). *Why Victims of Bullying Often Suffer in Silence*. Verywell Family; https://www.verywellfamily.com/reasons-why-victims-of-bullying-do-not-tell-460784

Gordon, S. (2014, February 27). *8 Reasons Why Teens Bully Others*. Verywell Family; https://www.verywellfamily.com/reasons-why-teens-bully-others-460532

Gordon, S. (2020a, May 26). *How Workplace Bullies Pick Their Targets*. Verywell Mind. https://www.verywellmind.com/reasons-why-workplace-bullies-target-people-460783

Gordon, S. (2020b, June 18). *Laying Down the Law for Cyberbullying*. Verywell Family. https://www.verywellfamily.com/cyberbullying-laws-4588306

Greenberg, M. (2015, December 6). *The 3 Most Common Causes of Insecurity and How to Beat Them.* Psychology Today. https://www.psychologytoday.com/gb/blog/the-mindful-self-express/201512/the-3-most-common-causes-insecurity-and-how-beat-them

Gregoire, C. (2014, September 26). *6 Reasons To Step Outside Your Comfort Zone.* HuffPost Canada; https://www.huffpost.com/entry/stepping-outside-your-comfort-zone_n_5872638

Guest, R. (2017, September 27). *7 Reasons Why Stepping Outside Your Comfort Zone is a Must.* Royston Guest. https://www.roystonguest.com/blog/7-reasons-why-stepping-outside-your-comfort-zone-is-a-must/

Harris, E. (2020). *What to Say to a Bully: 31 Expert Recommendations.* Crisis Prevention Institute. https://www.crisisprevention.com/Blog/What-to-Say-to-a-Bully

Herrera, V. (2013, February 2). *Loving the Person in the Mirror.* Rappler. https://www.rappler.com/life-and-style/loving-the-person-in-the-mirror

Hogan, B. (2021). *How to Be Proud of Yourself (and Why It's So Important).* Weight Watchers. https://www.weightwatchers.com/ca/en/article/how-be-proud-yourself-and-why-its-so-important

How to Create a Personal Mind Map: a Complete Guide. (2021). MindMaster. https://www.mindmaster.io/article/personal-mind-map.html

REFERENCES

How to Deal with Bullies. (n.d.). STOMP out Bullying. https://www.stompoutbullying.org/how-to-deal-with-bullies

How to Improve Self Confidence and 5 Mistakes to Avoid. (2018, September 27). Runrun.it Blog. https://blog.runrun.it/en/how-to-improve-self-confidence/

How To Mind Map Yourself For Growth. (2021). MindMaps Unleashed. https://mindmapsunleashed.com/how-to-mind-map-yourself-for-growth

https://www.facebook.com/verywell. (2019). *Protect Your Kids: Don't Be Duped by These Common Myths About Bullying.* Verywell Family. https://www.verywellfamily.com/common-myths-and-misconceptions-about-bullying-460490

Jacobson, S. (2016, January 12). *Assumptions - Why They Are Wrecking Your Mood and How To Stop Making Them.* Harley Therapy™ Blog. https://www.harleytherapy.co.uk/counselling/making-assumptions.htm

John, S. (2020, September 11). *The Key to Happiness is to be the Best Version of Yourself, and the Only Person in Control of That is You.* We Heart. https://www.we-heart.com/2020/09/11/creating-a-you-that-you-can-be-proud-of/

Kanaat, R. (2012). *48 Famous Failures Who Will Inspire You To Achieve.* Wanderlust Worker. https://www.wanderlustworker.com/48-famous-failures-who-will-inspire-you-to-achieve/

Karnaze, M. (2009, December 25). *How to Work With Your Emotions*. Mindful Construct. http://mindfulconstruct.com/how-to-work-with-your-emotions/

Kesarovska, L. (2013, April 14). *Building Self-Confidence with The Mirror Technique*. Let's Reach Success. https://letsreachsuccess.com/2013/04/14/talking-to-the-mirror-building-self-confidence/

Knight, C. (2018, April 12). *Dealing with Adult Bullying*. The Psych Professionals. https://psychprofessionals.com.au/dealing-adult-bullies/

Levis, J. (2019, December 17). *How to Stand Your Ground and Still Be Nice*. KiwiReport. https://www.kiwireport.com/stand-ground-still-nice/

MacKay, J. (2019, March 5). *5 Science-Backed Ways To Quiet Your Inner Perfectionist*. RescueTime Blog. https://blog.rescuetime.com/overcoming-perfectionism/

Makwana, B., Lee, Y., Parkin, S., & Farmer, L. (2018). *Selfie-Esteem: The Relationship Between Body Dissatisfaction and Social Media in Adolescent and Young Women*. In-Mind. https://www.in-mind.org/article/selfie-esteem-the-relationship-between-body-dissatisfaction-and-social-media-in-adolescent?gclid=EAIaIQobChMIsbSsxLTB7wIVrIBQBh2d8wMwEAAYAyAAEgLF5vD_BwE

Marinos, S. (2016, June 17). *6 Steps to Better Body Image*. Bodyandsoulau; https://www.bodyandsoul.com.au/diet/

body-confidence/6-steps-to-better-body-image/news-story/59c6fe2456a1a3e2c933d8ea0e2fd668

Marsh, J. (2011). *Tips for Keeping a Gratitude Journal*. Greater Good. https://greatergood.berkeley.edu/article/item/tips_for_keeping_a_gratitude_journal

Martin, S. (2017, May 8). *Why Highly Successful People Struggle With Low Self-Worth (and How You Can Reclaim Your Self-Worth)*. Psych Central. https://psychcentral.com/blog/imperfect/2017/05/why-highly-successful-people-struggle-with-low-self-worth#Success-can-never-cure-low-self-worth

Martinuzzi, B. (2013, August 30). *8 Ways Highly Successful People Overcome Self-Doubt*. Business Trends and Insights. https://www.americanexpress.com/en-us/business/trends-and-insights/articles/8-ways-highly-successful-people-overcome-self-doubt/

Maryville University. (2019, February 15). *Cyberbullying Definitions, Facts, Laws & Resources*. Maryville Online. https://online.maryville.edu/blog/what-is-cyberbullying-an-overview-for-students-parents-and-teachers/

Megraoui, B. (2019, April 26). *5 Easy Tips to Boost Your Low Self-Esteem While at University*. Top Universities. https://www.topuniversities.com/blog/5-easy-tips-boost-your-low-self-esteem-while-university

Meyers, S. (2012, January 9). *The Psychology of Why Celebrities Often Have Low Self-Esteem*. Psychology Today. https://www.psychologytoday.com/gb/blog/insight-is-2020/

201201/the-psychology-why-celebrities-often-have-low-self-esteem

Mind. (2019). *About Self-Esteem*. Mind. https://www.mind.org.uk/information-support/types-of-mental-health-problems/self-esteem/about-self-esteem/

Mind Mapping Basics. (2017). SimpleMind. https://simplemind.eu/how-to-mind-map/basics/

Mind Tools Content Team. (n.d.). *Developing "Character": Learning How to Stand Your Ground*. Mind Tools. https://www.mindtools.com/pages/article/newCS_81.htm

Morin, A. (2018, June 24). *How to Change That Negative Voice in Your Head*. Psychology Today. https://www.psychologytoday.com/gb/blog/what-mentally-strong-people-dont-do/201806/how-change-negative-voice-in-your-head

Morin, A. (2019a). *5 Ways to Start Boosting Your Self-Confidence Today*. Verywell Mind. https://www.verywellmind.com/how-to-boost-your-self-confidence-4163098

Morin, A. (2019b). *The Truth About How Many People Are Bullied at School and at Work*. Verywell Family. https://www.verywellfamily.com/bullying-statistics-to-know-4589438

Myhre, S. (2021). *Safety Behaviors | Austin Anxiety Therapists*. Austin Anxiety. https://www.austinanxiety.com/safety-behaviors/

National Eating Disorders Association. (2018, February 22). *10 Steps to Positive Body Image*. National Eating Disorders

Association. https://www.nationaleatingdisorders.org/learn/general-information/ten-steps

Newport Academy. (2018, September 6). *How to Cultivate Positive Teen Body Image.* Newport Academy. https://www.newportacademy.com/resources/well-being/teen-body-image/#:~:text=Increased%20self%2Dacceptance%3A%20A%20positive

Ni, P. (2016). *8 Keys to Handling Adult Bullies.* Psychology Today. https://www.psychologytoday.com/us/blog/communication-success/201611/8-keys-handling-adult-bullies

Page, O. (2020, November 4). *How to Leave your Comfort Zone and Enter your "Growth Zone."* PositivePsychology. https://positivepsychology.com/comfort-zone/

Plante, Thomas G. (2009). *Helping Others.* Psychology Today. https://www.psychologytoday.com/gb/blog/do-the-right-thing/200911/helping-others

Positive Psychology. (2019). Psychology Today. https://www.psychologytoday.com/us/basics/positive-psychology

Psychology Tools. (2021a). *Behavioral Experiment.* Psychology Tools. https://www.psychologytools.com/resource/behavioral-experiment/

Psychology Tools. (2021b). *Challenging Your Negative Thinking.* Psychology Tools. https://www.psychologytools.com/resource/challenging-your-negative-thinking/

Psychology Tools. (2021c). *Gratitude Journal*. Psychology Tools. https://www.psychologytools.com/resource/gratitude-journal/

Psychology Tools. (2021d). *What Do People Think About Themselves (CYP)?* Psychology Tools. https://www.psychologytools.com/resource/what-do-people-think-about-themselves-cyp/

Radha. (2021). *7 Stars Who Have Personal Experiences of Online Bullying*. BBC. https://www.bbc.co.uk/programmes/articles/3QcD9W13Dr0bxmt4CMWVkGk/7-stars-who-have-personal-experiences-of-online-bullying

Realbuzz Team. (n.d.). *8 Ways To Boost Your Body Confidence*. Realbuzz. https://www.realbuzz.com/articles-interests/health/article/8-ways-to-boost-body-confidence/

Rinkunas, S., & Creveling, M. (2018, June 19). *Repeating This Phrase Over And Over Will Make You Feel Like A Badass*. Women's Health. https://www.womenshealthmag.com/life/a19933675/boost-body-confidence/

Sammon, E. (2018, November 27). *Analyzing Comfort Zones*. Medium. https://medium.com/sojourners-heart/analyzing-comfort-zones-f5f178d30137

Sarah. (2019, June 28). *10 Things I'm Doing To Be More Confident*. Proud Happy Brave. https://proud-happy-brave.com/be-more-confident/

Self Confidence. (2016, August 15). Cleverism. https://www.cleverism.com/skills-and-tools/self-confidence/#:~:text=Self%2Dconfidence%20is%20a%20skill

Selig, M. (2019, June 17). *Is Confidence a Skill You Can Learn?* Psychology Today. https://www.psychologytoday.com/gb/blog/changepower/201906/is-confidence-skill-you-can-learn

Seunagal, G. (2021, February 2). *How To Handle Adult Bullying.* BetterHelp. https://www.betterhelp.com/advice/bullying/how-to-handle-adult-bullying/

Shah, F. (2018, September 15). *Building One's Motivation.* The Positive Psychology People. https://www.thepositivepsychologypeople.com/building-ones-motivation/

Shore, K. (2019). *The Student with Low Self-Esteem.* Educationworld.com. https://www.educationworld.com/a_curr/shore/shore059.shtml

Shutterfly Community. (2018, July 3). *How to Start a Gratitude Journal You'll Actually Keep.* Shutterfly. https://www.shutterfly.com/ideas/how-to-start-a-gratitude-journal/

Sicinski, A. (2013, July 8). *Practical Ideas to Help You Quickly Improve Your Self-Esteem.* IQ Matrix Blog. https://blog.iqmatrix.com/improve-self-esteem

Simpkin, T. (2020, January 8). *Mixed Feelings: How to Deal With Emotions at Work.* Totaljobs. https://www.totaljobs.com/advice/emotions-at-work

Singh, A. (2019, January 24). *Mind your Mindset.* Medium. https://medium.com/@ummerr/mind-your-mindset-d9df92a1de0d

Smart, J. Y. (2016, December 12). *Get Smart: Why Students Keep Bullying a Secret.* Savannah Morning News. https://www.savannahnow.com/accent-column/2016-12-12/get-smart-why-students-keep-bullying-secret

Smith, C. (2014, November 10). *Overcoming Low Self-Esteem with Mindfulness.* Psychology Today. https://www.psychologytoday.com/gb/blog/shift/201411/overcoming-low-self-esteem-mindfulness

Smith, R., Alkozei, A., & Killgore, W. D. S. (2017). How Do Emotions Work? *Frontiers for Young Minds, 5.* https://doi.org/10.3389/frym.2017.00069

Star, C. (2017, September 3). *Boundaries: Learn How to Stand Your Ground.* Psych Central. https://psychcentral.com/blog/boundaries-learn-how-to-stand-your-ground#1

Stretch, R. (2016, August 30). *How to Make Mind Maps: Visualize Your Ideas for Better Brainstorming.* Zapier. https://zapier.com/blog/mind-mapping-tutorial/

Styzek, K. (2021, April 21). *How to Ignore People Who Try to Pick on You.* WikiHow. https://www.wikihow.com/Ignore-People-Who-Try-to-Pick-on-You

The Art of Saying No: How to Stand Your Ground. (2015, May 28). Loren's World. https://www.lorensworld.com/business/life-work/the-art-of-saying-no-how-to-stand-your-ground/

The Importance of Mindset. (2011). SkillsYouNeed. https://www.skillsyouneed.com/ps/mindsets.html

Tips to Improve Your Self-Esteem. (2021). Mind. https://www.mind.org.uk/information-support/types-of-mental-health-problems/self-esteem/tips-to-improve-your-self-esteem/?gclid=EAIaIQobChMIzZWFwKDB7wIVzOvtCh3X0gqWEAAYAyAAEgJ0vfD_BwE

Uche, U. (2012, October 8). *Putting an End to Bullying Without Bullying.* Psychology Today. https://www.psychologytoday.com/gb/blog/promoting-empathy-your-teen/201210/putting-end-bullying-without-bullying

Vermeer-Quist, H. (2020, April 17). *Ground Yourself in Faith Using Positive Psychology as a Tool.* Faithward. https://www.faithward.org/ground-in-faith-positive-psych/

Whalley, D. M. (2019). *Low Self-Esteem.* Psychology Tools. https://www.psychologytools.com/self-help/low-self-esteem/

Woman and Home. (2016, November 16). *Top 10 Tips For Body Confidence.* Woman&Home. https://www.womanandhome.com/health-and-wellbeing/top-10-tips-for-body-confidence-90804/

York, U. of. (n.d.). *Low Self Esteem.* University of York. https://www.york.ac.uk/students/health/advice/self-esteem/

IMAGE REFERENCES

Figure 1: Map. From Pixabay, by Clker-Free-Vector-Images, 2014. https://pixabay.com/vectors/map-navigation-geography-312213/

Figure 2: Who You Are. From Unsplash, by Motoki Tonn, 2019. https://unsplash.com/photos/GuCdEgE3Gcw

Figure 3: Two is a Crowd. From Pixabay, by Yuu Khoang, 2019. https://pixabay.com/illustrations/leaves-branch-circuit-plant-4170606/

Figure 4: Self-Confidence and Self-Esteem. From Unsplash, by Robert Stump, 2021. https://unsplash.com/photos/RQ35cS1OpPA

Figure 5: Mandala 1. From Pixabay, by Kaylin Art, 2017. https://pixabay.com/illustrations/drawing-mandala-design-cool-2151087/

Figure 6: Cyberbullying. From Pixabay, by Kirill Sharkovski, 2019. https://unsplash.com/photos/YaqTssZ-GZk

Figure 7: Stay Quiet. From Pixabay, by Prawny, 2021. https://pixabay.com/illustrations/butterflies-vintage-sketch-insects-5998763/

Figure 8: Not Alone. From Pixabay, by Victoria_Borodinova, 2020. https://pixabay.com/illustrations/eyes-sketch-fantasy-open-fear-5498877/

Figure 9: Mandala 2. From Pixabay, by Kaylin Art, 2017. https://pixabay.com/illustrations/flowers-mandala-hand-drawing-2147877/

Figure 10: Boundaries. From Unsplash, by Hello I'm Nik, 2017. https://unsplash.com/photos/MAgPyHRO0AA

Figure 11: Mindfulness. From Unsplash, by Mathew Schwartz, 2018. https://unsplash.com/photos/3SWQCLmxH1U

Figure 12: Gratitude Journal. From Pixabay, by Emmie_Norfolk, 2020. https://pixabay.com/illustrations/vintage-decor-vine-flower-leaf-4938443/

Figure 13: Mind Map. From Pixabay, by Media Modifier, 2020. https://pixabay.com/illustrations/mind-mapping-icon-thinking-mind-map-5597528/

Figure 14: Your Body. From Unsplash, by Mahdi Dastmard, 2019. https://unsplash.com/photos/kizxaWXl-i0

Figure 15: Outside Your Safety Net. From Pixabay, by GDJ, 2020. https://pixabay.com/vectors/seashell-drawing-shell-snail-5556083/

Figure 16: Steps to Take. From Pixabay, by Emmie_Norfolk, 2020. https://pixabay.com/illustrations/vintage-decor-vine-flower-leaf-4938370/

Figure 17: Mindset. From Pixabay, by Gordon Johnson, 2017. https://pixabay.com/vectors/a-i-ai-anatomy-2729794/

Figure 18: You Wake Me Up. From Pixabay, by Mike Renpening, 2018. https://pixabay.com/vectors/stand-up-wake-up-wake-up-3200284/

Figure 19: Proud of Yourself. From Pixabay, by Gordon Johnson, 2016. https://pixabay.com/vectors/woman-female-girl-human-person-1801281/

Figure 20: Freedom. From Pixabay, by Clker-Free-Vector-Images, 2014. https://pixabay.com/vectors/freedom-jump-reach-silhouettes-307791/

Made in the USA
Las Vegas, NV
28 September 2023